ID # 3146 CLS

W9-BGB-416

Introduction *to* Great Books

THIRD 3 SERIES

The Great Books Foundation

A nonprofit educational corporation

Published and distributed by

The Great Books Foundation
A Nonprofit Educational Corporation
35 East Wacker Drive, Suite 400
Chicago, Illinois 60601

Formerly published as Junior Great Books Series Twelve

Acknowledgments

All possible care has been taken to trace ownership and secure permission for each selection in this series. The Great Books Foundation wishes to thank the following authors, publishers, and representatives for permission to reprint copyright material:

On Happiness from RHETORIC, translated by W. Rhys Roberts, in THE WORKS OF ARISTOTLE edited by W. D. Ross, reprinted by permission of Oxford University Press; and NICOMACHEAN ETHICS, translated by Martin Ostwald, copyright © 1962 by Bobbs-Merrill Educational Publishing, by permission of the publisher.

Habits and Will from HUMAN NATURE AND CONDUCT by John Dewey. Reprinted with the permission of the Center for Dewey Studies, Southern Illinois University at Carbondale.

Happiness from HAPPINESS by Mary Lavin. Copyright © 1969 by Mary Lavin. By permission of Wallace & Sheil Agency, Inc.

Crito from PLATO: THE LAST DAYS OF SOCRATES, pages 79-96, translated by Hugh Tredennick. Copyright © 1954, 1959, 1969 by Hugh Tredennick. Reprinted by permission of Penguin Books Ltd.

Conscience from LECTURES ON ETHICS by Immanuel Kant, translated by Louis Infield. Published by Methuen and Co., Ltd, 1930. By permission of Associated Book Publishers Ltd.

A Hunger Artist from FRANZ KAFKA: THE COMPLETE STORIES, edited by Nahum N. Glatzer. Copyright © 1948, 1971 by Schocken Books Inc. Reprinted by permission of Shocken Books Inc.

Antigone from THE ANTIGONE OF SOPHOCLES: An English Version by Dudley Fitts and Robert Fitzgerald. Copyright 1939 by Harcourt Brace Jovanovich, Inc.; renewed 1967 by Dudley Fitts and Robert Fitzgerald. Reprinted by permission of the publisher.
CAUTION: All rights, including professional, amateur, motion picture, recitation, lecturing, performance, public reading, radio broadcasting, and television are strictly reserved. Inquiries on all rights should be addressed to Harcourt Brace Jovanovich, Inc., 757 Third Avenue, New York 10017.

Why Great Revolutions Will Become Rare from DEMOCRACY IN AMERICA by Alexis de Tocqueville, a new translation by George Lawrence, edited by J. P. Mayer and Max Lerner. Copyright © 1966 in the English translation by Harper & Row, Publisher, Inc. Reprinted by permission of the publisher.

A Room of One's Own from A ROOM OF ONE'S OWN by Virginia Woolf. Copyright 1929 by Harcourt Brace Jovanovich, Inc.; renewed 1957 by Leonard Woolf. Reprinted by permission of the publisher.

In Dreams Begin Responsibilities from IN DREAMS BEGIN RESPONSIBILITIES by Delmore Schwartz. Copyright © 1978 by New Directions Publishing Corporation. Reprinted by permission of New Directions.

Contents

UNIT

I
p. 1

Shared Inquiry
On Happiness √
Aristotle

II
p. 11

Great Writers
Habits and Will *Sept. 23*
John Dewey

III
p. 27

What a Story Is
Happiness *Sept. 16*
Mary Lavin

IV
p. 51

Crito *Oct. 7*
Plato
Preparing for Discussion

V
p. 71

Interpretation
On Liberty
John Stuart Mill

VI
p. 89

Conscience
Immanuel Kant
Questions of Fact,
Interpretation, and Evaluation

Sept 30

Getting Into a Story
A Hunger Artist
Franz Kafka

VII
p. 103

Of the Limits of Government
Oct. 21
John Locke
Developing Interpretive Questions

VIII
p. 121

Interpretive questions

Antigone
Sophocles
Practice: Writing Interpretive Questions

IX
p. 135

Why Great Revolutions Will Become Rare
Alexis de Tocqueville

X
p. 189

Oct. 14
A Room of One's Own
Virginia Woolf

XI
p. 211

Oct. 28
In Dreams Begin Responsibilities
Delmore Schwartz

XII
p. 233

I

Shared Inquiry

A Great Books discussion explores the meaning of a selection that everyone in the group has read in advance. Discussion begins with a leader's interpretive question—a question about a problem of meaning that interests her in the selection. After reading the selection carefully, she has no answer to her question or she thinks that her question can be answered in more than one way. In either case, she wants to explore it with the group. Because leaders and group members work together to try to resolve such problems of meaning, we call the method of discussion *shared inquiry*.

As you discuss the problem, the leader will ask questions for several purposes: to help you clarify your remarks or support your answers with evidence from the selection, to make sure everyone will be given a chance to offer opinions, and to keep discussion moving toward a resolution of the problem.

As a group member, you need not wait to be called on. You may speak up at any time. You may respond directly to other group members as well as to the leader. You may express agreement or disagreement with what others say, add your own thoughts, or ask questions related to the problem being discussed. If you are called on but have nothing to say at the moment, you are equally free not to answer. If you have an idea that you are unsure of, or if you don't know whether your idea is a good one, don't be afraid to express it anyway—it may prove more valuable than you think.

To encourage group members to think for themselves and to guarantee that no one is excluded from discussion, shared inquiry has four rules:

1. **No one may take part in the discussion without first reading the selection.** If you have not read the selection, you cannot contribute to the discussion because you are unprepared to offer opinions and to support them with evidence from the selection.

2. **Discuss only the selection that everyone has read.** If you refer to other essays or stories, the participants who have not read them will be denied a chance to contribute to the discussion. This rule also enables the group to check the validity of what is said by referring to the assigned selection.

3. **Do not introduce outside opinions unless you can back them up with evidence from the selection.** If you get an idea about the meaning of a selection from an outside source—for example, the opinion of someone you know or an insight from another book—you may use the idea in discussion only if you can express it in your own words and support it with evidence from the selection.

4. **Leaders may only ask questions—they may not answer them.** If leaders stated their own opinions about the meaning of a selection, you might feel less inclined to think for yourself. You might also be less likely to believe that other equally good answers were possible. As a participant you are not limited to offering answers; you may ask questions, too. ▮▮

By and About Aristotle

(384–322 B.C.)

Aristotle said that philosophy grew out of wonder:

> It is owing to their wonder that men both now begin and first began to philosophize. They wondered originally at the obvious difficulties, then advanced little by little and stated difficulties about the greater matters, e.g., about the phenomena of the moon and those of the sun and of the stars, and about the genesis of the universe. And a man who is puzzled and wonders thinks himself ignorant (whence even the lover of myth is in a sense a lover of Wisdom, for the myth is composed of wonders); therefore since they philosophized in order to escape from ignorance, evidently they were pursuing science in order to know, and not for any utilitarian end.

His own curiosity ranged wide. He wrote on the importance of experience in scientific investigation:

> Lack of experience diminishes our power of taking a comprehensive view of the admitted facts. Hence those who dwell in intimate association with nature and its phenomena grow more and more able to formulate, as the foundations of their theories, principals such as to admit of a wider and coherent development, while those whom devotion to abstract discussions has rendered unobservant of the facts are too ready to dogmatize on the basis of a few observations.

On the policy of tyrants:

> Their first end and aim is to break the spirit of their subjects; they know that a poor-spirited man will never plot against anybody. Their second aim is to breed mutual distrust. Tyranny is never overthrown until men begin to trust one another, and this is the reason why tyrants are always at outs with the good. They feel that good men are doubly dangerous to their authority—dangerous, first, in thinking it shame to be governed as if they were slaves; dangerous, again, in their spirit of mutual and general loyalty and in their refusal to betray one another or anyone else. The third and last aim of tyrants is to make their subjects incapable of action.

Nobody attempts the impossible. Nobody, therefore, will attempt the overthrow of a tyranny when all are incapable of action.

On age and youth:

Elderly men . . . have lived many years; they have often been taken in and often made mistakes; and life on the whole is a bad business. The result is that they are sure about nothing and under-do everything. They "think," but they never "know"; and because of their hesitation they always add a "possibly" or a "perhaps," putting everything this way and nothing positively. They are cynical; that is, they tend to put the worse construction on everything. Further, their experience makes them distrustful and therefore suspicious of evil. Consequently they neither love warmly nor hate bitterly, but . . . love as though they will some day hate and hate as though they will some day love.

Young men . . . would always rather do noble deeds than useful ones. Their lives are regulated more by moral feeling than by reasoning, and whereas reasoning leads us to choose what is useful, moral goodness leads us to choose what is noble. They are fonder of their friends, intimates, and companions than older men are because they like spending their days in the company of others and have not yet come to value either their friends or anything else by their usefulness to themselves. All their mistakes are in the direction of doing things excessiely and vehemently. . . . They think they know everything, and are always quite sure about it; this in fact, is why they overdo everything. . . . They are fond of fun and therefore witty, wit being well-bred insolence.

In the following selections from *Rhetoric* and *Nicomachean Ethics,* Aristotle discusses happiness. Because he believes that every time we choose something we do so because we think it will help make us happy, he considers happiness the highest good. It is, therefore, important to know what happiness is: as Aristotle asks in the *Ethics,* "Will not the knowledge of it have a great influence on our lives? Would we not, like archers who have a target to aim at, be more likely to hit the proper mark?"

On Happiness

Aristotle

It may be said that every individual man and all men in common aim at a certain end which determines what they choose and what they avoid. This end, to sum it up briefly, is happiness and its constituents. Let us, then, by way of illustration only, ascertain what is in general the nature of happiness, and what are the elements of its constituent parts. For all advice to do things or not to do them is concerned with happiness and with the things that make for or against it; whatever creates or increases happiness or some part of happiness, we ought to do; whatever destroys or hampers happiness, or gives rise to its opposite, we ought not to do.

We may define happiness as prosperity combined with virtue; or as independence of life; or as the secure enjoyment of the maximum of pleasure; or as a good condition of property and body, together with the power of guarding one's property and body and making use of them. That happiness is one or more of these things, pretty well everybody agrees.

---

*A selection from *Rhetoric* and *Nicomachean Ethics*.

From this definition of happiness it follows that its constituent parts are: good birth, plenty of friends, good friends, wealth, good children, plenty of children, a happy old age, also such bodily excellences as health, beauty, strength, large stature, athletic powers, together with fame, honor, good luck, and virtue. A man cannot fail to be completely independent if he possesses these internal and these external goods; for besides these there are no others to have. (Goods of the soul and of the body are internal. Good birth, friends, money, and honor are external.) Further, we think that he should possess resources and luck, in order to make his life really secure. . . .

To call happiness the highest good is perhaps a little trite, and a clearer account of what it is is still required. Perhaps this is best done by first ascertaining the proper function of man. For just as the goodness and performance of a flute player, a sculptor, or any kind of expert, and generally of anyone who fulfills some function or performs some action, are thought to reside in his proper function, so the goodness and performance of man would seem to reside in whatever is his proper function. Is it then possible that while a carpenter and a shoemaker have their own proper functions and spheres of action, man as man has none, but was left by nature a good-for-nothing without a function? Should we not assume that just as the eye, the hand, the foot, and in general each part of the body clearly has its own proper function, so man too has some function over and above the functions of his parts? What can this function possibly be? Simply living? He shares that even with plants, but we are now looking for something peculiar to man. Accordingly, the life of nutrition and growth must be excluded. Next in line there is a life of sense perception. But this, too, man has in common with the horse, the ox, and every animal. There remains then an active life of the rational element. The rational element has two parts: one is rational in that it obeys the rule of reason, the other in that it possesses and conceives rational rules. Since the expression "life of the rational element" also can be used in two senses, we must make it clear that we mean a life determined by the activity, as opposed to the mere possession, of the rational element. For the activity, it seems, has a greater claim to be the function of man.

The proper function of man, then, consists in an activity of the soul in conformity with a rational principle or, at least, not without it. In speaking of the proper function of a given individual we mean that it is the same in kind as the function of an individual who sets high standards for himself: the proper function of a harpist, for example, is the same as the function of a harpist who has set high standards for himself. The same applies to any and every group of individuals: the full attainment of excellence must be added to the mere function. In other words, the function of the harpist is to play the harp; the function of the harpist who has high standards is to play it well. On these assumptions, if we take the proper function of man to be a certain kind of life, and if this kind of life is an activity of the soul and consists in actions performed in conjunction with the rational element, and if a man of high standards is he who performs these actions well and properly, and if a function is well performed when it is performed in accordance with the excellence appropriate to it; we reach the conclusion that the good of man is an activity of the soul in conformity with excellence or virtue, and if there are several virtues, in conformity with the best and most complete.

But we must add "in a complete life." For one swallow does not make a spring, nor does one sunny day; similarly, one day or a short time does not make a man blessed and happy.

Interpretive Questions

1. Is a good person automatically happy, according to Aristotle?

2. According to the *Ethics,* does being happy depend entirely upon yourself?

3. Does Aristotle think happiness is possible for everyone?

4. Does a person need all of the constituent parts of happiness to be happy?

5. Can happiness be obtained without effort, according to Aristotle?

II

Great Writers

Reading what Thucydides has to say about the
relationship between great powers and their
satellites, or what Thomas Hobbes has to say
about human nature and government, or what
John Dewey has to say about the formation of
habits can change the way we look at things. We
may not agree with these writers, but as we come
to understand what they say, it is unlikely that we
will ever again think about foreign policy or
government or habit in quite the same way.

This kind of writing is rare. The depth of thought it conveys often makes it difficult to understand. We need to work hard to make a great writer's ideas our own. For making an idea our own is not a simple matter of agreement or memorization. It means becoming so familiar with someone else's thought that we can turn it around, consider it from different angles, and then decide how it fits with our own ideas.

Great writers give us the opportunity to form our own opinions on the basis of the most profound thinking that has ever been expressed. They require us to think about what it means to live in the world and about what we are and what we hope to become. As we make an effort to understand great writers, we find ourselves seeing further, as Isaac Newton put it, "by standing upon the shoulders of giants." ▮▮

By and About John Dewey

(1859–1952)

John Dewey viewed philosophy as a means of studying the problems that arise in everyday life. About experience, Dewey wrote:

> We always live at the time we live and not at some other time, and only by extracting at each present time the full meaning of each present experience are we prepared for doing the same thing in the future. This is the only preparation which in the long run amounts to anything.

> With the animals, an experience perishes as it happens, and each new doing or suffering stands alone. But man lives in a world where each occurrence is charged with echoes and reminiscences of what has gone before, where each event is a reminder of other things. Hence he lives not, like the beasts of the field, in a world of merely physical things but in a world of signs and symbols. A stone is not merely hard, a thing into which one bumps; but it is a monument of a deceased ancestor. A flame is not merely something which warms or burns, but is a symbol of the enduring life of the household.

On specialized education:

> Almost everyone has had occasion to look back upon his school days and wonder what has become of the knowledge he was supposed to have amassed during his years of schooling, and why it is that the technical skills he acquired have to be learned over again in changed form in order to stand him in good stead. One trouble is that the subject matter in question was learned in isolation; it was put, as it were, in a water-tight compartment. When the question is asked, then, what has become of it, where has it gone to, the right answer is that it is still there in the special compartment in which it was originally stowed away. If exactly the same conditions recurred as those under which it was acquired, it would also recur and be available. But it was segregated when it was acquired and hence is so disconnected from the rest of experience that it is not available under the actual conditions of life.

On freedom:

> The only freedom that is of enduring importance is freedom of intelligence, that is to say, freedom of observation and of judgment exercised in behalf of purposes that are intrinsically worthwhile.

On the uses of intelligence:

> Intelligence is not something possessed once for all. It is in constant process of forming, and its retention requires constant alertness in observing consequences, an open-minded will to learn, and courage in readjustment.

> The story of the achievement of science in physical control is evidence of the possibility of control in social affairs. It is our human intelligence and human courage which are on trial; it is incredible that men who have brought the technique of physical discovery, invention, and use to such a pitch of perfection will abdicate in the face of the infinitely more important human problem.

In Human Nature and Conduct, *John Dewey says that our moral life is more complex than we suspect: impulse, habit, and intelligence are all part of it. According to Dewey, the impulses each of us is born with would lead to blind, chaotic activity if left to themselves; but society steps in to channel our impulses with its demands and customs, and we learn habits of conduct. However, these habits are constantly being challenged—by other habits, by desires, by novel situations—and when habit is blocked, blind impulse waits, ready to take over. If we are to avoid being dominated by either stubborn habit or blind impulse, our intelligence must intervene, striking a balance between the two. In our selection, Dewey discusses the power of habit and the part it plays in setting and achieving goals.*

Habits and Will

John Dewey

It is a significant fact that in order to appreciate the peculiar place of habit in activity we have to betake ourselves to bad habits: foolish idling, gambling, addiction to liquor and drugs. When we think of such habits, the union of habit with desire and with propulsive power is forced upon us. When we think of habits in terms of walking, playing a musical instrument, typewriting, we are much given to thinking of habits as technical abilities existing apart from our likings and as lacking in urgent impulsion. We think of them as passive tools waiting to be called into action from without. A bad habit suggests an inherent tendency to action and also a hold, a command over us. It makes us do things we are ashamed of, things which we tell ourselves we prefer not to do. It overrides our formal resolutions, our conscious decisions. When we are honest with ourselves we acknowledge that a habit has this power because it is so intimately a part of ourselves. It has a hold upon us because we are the habit.

---

*A selection from *Human Nature and Conduct*.

17

Our self-love, our refusal to face facts, combined perhaps with a sense of a possible better although unrealized self, leads us to eject the habit from the thought of ourselves and conceive it as an evil power which has somehow overcome us. We feed our conceit by recalling that the habit was not deliberately formed; we never intended to become idlers or gamblers or roués. And how can anything be deeply ourselves which developed accidentally, without set intentions? These traits of a bad habit are precisely the things which are most instructive about all habits and about ourselves. They teach us that all habits are affections, that all have projectile power, and that a predisposition formed by a number of specific acts is an immensely more intimate and fundamental part of ourselves than are vague, general, conscious choices. All habits are demands for certain kinds of activity; and they constitute the self. In any intelligible sense of the word *will*, they *are* will. They form our effective desires and they furnish us with our working capacities. They rule our thoughts, determining which shall appear and be strong and which shall pass from light into obscurity.

We may think of habits as means, waiting, like tools in a box, to be used by conscious resolve. But they are something more than that. They are active means, means that project themselves, energetic and dominating ways of acting. We need to distinguish between materials, tools, and means proper. Nails and boards are not, strictly speaking, means of a box. They are only materials for making it. Even the saw and hammer are means only when they are employed in some actual making. Otherwise, they are tools, or potential means. They are actual means only when brought in conjunction with eye, arm, and hand in some specific operation. And eye, arm, and hand are, correspondingly, means proper only when they are in active operation. And whenever they are in action they are cooperating with external materials and energies. Without support from beyond themselves, the eye stares blankly and the hand moves fumblingly. They are means only when they enter into organization with things which independently accomplish definite results. These organizations are habits. . . .

Recently a friend remarked to me that there was one superstition current among even cultivated persons. They suppose that if one is told what to do, if the right *end* is pointed to them, all that is required in order to bring about the right act is will or wish on the part of the one who is to act. He used as an illustration the matter of physical posture; the assumption is that if a man is told to stand up straight, all that is further needed is wish and effort on his part, and the deed is done. He pointed out that this belief is on a par with primitive magic in its neglect of attention to the means which are involved in reaching an end. And he went on to say that the prevalence of this belief, starting with false notions about the control of the body and extending to control of mind and character, is the greatest bar to intelligent social progress. It bars the way because it makes us neglect intelligent inquiry to discover the means which will produce a desired result, and intelligent invention to procure the means. In short, it leaves out the importance of intelligently controlled habit.

We may cite his illustration of the real nature of a physical aim or order and its execution in its contrast with the current false notion. A man who has a bad habitual posture tells himself, or is told, to stand up straight. If he is interested and responds, he braces himself, goes through certain movements, and it is assumed that the desired result is substantially attained; and that the position is retained at least as long as the man keeps the idea or order in his mind. Consider the assumptions which are here made. It is implied that the means or effective conditions of the realization of a purpose exist independently of established habit, and even that they may be set in motion in opposition to habit. It is assumed that means are there, so that the failure to stand erect is wholly a matter of failure of purpose and desire. It needs paralysis or a broken leg or some other equally gross phenomenon to make us appreciate the importance of objective conditions.

Now in fact a man who *can* stand properly does so, and only a man who can, does. In the former case, fiats of will are unnecessary, and in the latter useless. A man who does not stand properly forms a habit of standing improperly, a positive, forceful habit. The common implication that his mistake is merely negative, that he is simply failing to do the right thing, and that the failure can be made good by an order of will is absurd. One might as well suppose that the man who is a slave of whiskey-drinking is merely one who fails to drink water. Conditions have been formed for producing a bad result, and the bad result will occur as long as those conditions exist. They can no more be dismissed by a direct effort of will than the conditions which create drought can be dispelled by whistling for wind. It is as reasonable to expect a fire to go out when it is ordered to stop burning as to suppose that a man can stand straight in consequence of a direct action of thought and desire. The fire can be put out only by changing objective conditions; it is the same with rectification of bad posture.

Of course something happens when a man acts upon his idea of standing straight. For a little while he stands differently, but only a different kind of badly. He then takes the unaccustomed feeling which accompanies his unusual stand as evidence that he is now standing right. But there are many ways of standing badly, and he has simply shifted his usual way to a compensatory bad way at some opposite extreme. When we realize this fact, we are likely to suppose that it exists because control of the *body* is physical and hence is external to mind and will. Transfer the command inside character and mind, and it is fancied that an idea of an end and the desire to realize it will take immediate effect. After we get to the point of recognizing that habits must intervene between wish and execution in the case of bodily acts, we still cherish the illusion that they can be dispensed with in the case of mental and moral acts. Thus the net result is to make us sharpen the distinction between non-moral and moral activities and to lead us to confine the latter strictly within a private, immaterial realm. But in fact, formation of ideas as well as their execution depends upon habit. *If* we could form a correct idea without a correct habit, then possibly we could carry it out irrespective of habit. But a wish gets definite form only in connection with an idea, and an idea gets shape and consistency only when it has a habit back of it. Only when a man can already perform an act of standing straight does he know what it is like to have a right posture, and only then can he summon the idea required for proper execution. The act must come before the thought, and a habit before an ability to evoke the thought at will. Ordinary psychology reverses the actual state of affairs....

Only the man who can maintain a correct posture has the stuff out of which to form that idea of standing erect which can be the starting point of a right act. Only the man whose habits are already good can know what the good is. Immediate, seemingly instinctive, feeling of the direction and end of various lines of behavior is in reality the feeling of habits working below direct consciousness. The psychology of illusions of perception is full of illustrations of the distortion introduced by habit into observation of objects. The same fact accounts for the intuitive element in judgments of action, an element which is valuable or the reverse in accord with the quality of dominant habits. For, as Aristotle remarked, the untutored moral perceptions of a good man are usually trustworthy, those of a bad character, not. (But he should have added that the influence of social custom as well as personal habit has to be taken into account in estimating who is the good man and the good judge.)

What is true of the dependence of execution of an idea upon habit is true, then, of the formation and quality of the idea. Suppose that by a happy chance a right concrete idea or purpose—concrete, not simply correct in words—has been hit upon: What happens when one with an incorrect habit tries to act in accord with it? Clearly the idea can be carried into execution only with a mechanism already there. If this is defective or perverted, the best intention in the world will yield bad results. In the case of no other engine does one suppose that a defective machine will turn out good goods simply because it is invited to. Everywhere else we recognize that the design and structure of the agency employed tell directly upon the work done. Given a bad habit and the "will" or mental direction to get a good result, and the actual happening is a reverse or looking-glass manifestation of the usual fault—a compensatory twist in the opposite direction. Refusal to recognize this fact only leads to a separation of mind from body, and to supposing that mental or "physical" mechanisms are different in kind from those of bodily operations and independent of them. So deep seated is this notion that even so "scientific" a theory as modern psychoanalysis thinks that mental habits can be straightened out by some kind of purely psychical manipulation without reference to the distortions of sensation and perception which are due to bad bodily sets. The other side of the error is found in the notion of "scientific" nerve physiologists that it is only necessary to locate a particular diseased cell or local lesion, independent of the whole complex or organic habits, in order to rectify conduct.

Means are means; they are intermediates, middle terms. To grasp this fact is to have done with the ordinary dualism of means and ends. The "end" is merely a series of acts viewed at a remote stage; and a means is merely the series viewed at an earlier one. The distinction of means and end arises in surveying the *course* of a proposed *line* of action, a connected series in time. The "end" is the last act thought of; the means are the acts to be performed prior to it in time. To *reach* an end we must take our mind off from it and attend to the act which is next to be performed. We must make that the end. The only exception to this statement is in cases where customary habit determines the course of the series. Then all that is wanted is a cue to set it off. But when the proposed end involves any deviation from usual action or any rectification of it—as in the case of standing straight—then the main thing is to find some act which is different from the usual one. The discovery and performance of this unaccustomed act is the "end" to which we must devote all attention. Otherwise we shall simply do the old thing over again, no matter what is our conscious command. The only way of accomplishing this discovery is through a flank movement. We must stop even thinking of standing up straight. To think of it is fatal, for it commits us to the operation of an established habit of standing wrong. We must find an act within our power which is disconnected from any thought about standing. We must start to do another thing which on one side inhibits our falling into the customary bad position and on the other side is the beginning of a series of acts which may lead into the correct posture. The hard-drinker who keeps thinking of not drinking is doing what he can to initiate the acts which lead to drinking. He is starting with the stimulus to his habit. To succeed he must find some positive interest or line of action which will inhibit the drinking series and which by instituting another course of action will bring him to his desired end. In short, the man's true aim is to discover some course of action, having nothing to do with the habit of drink or standing erect, which will take him where he wants to go. The discovery of this other series is at once his means and his end. Until one takes intermediate acts seriously enough to treat them as ends, one wastes one's time in any effort at change of habits. Of the intermediate acts, the most important is the *next* one. The first or earliest means is the most important *end* to discover.

Means and ends are two names for the same reality. The terms denote not a division in reality but a distinction in judgment. Without understanding this fact we cannot understand the nature of habits nor can we pass beyond the usual separation of the moral and non-moral in conduct. "End" is a name for a series of acts taken collectively—like the term army. "Means" is a name for the same series taken distributively— like this soldier, that officer. To think of the end signifies to extend and enlarge our view of the act to be performed. It means to look at the next act in perspective, not permitting it to occupy the entire field of vision. To bear the end in mind signifies that we should not stop thinking about our *next* act until we form some reasonably clear idea of the *course* of action to which it commits us. To attain a remote end means, on the other hand, to treat the end as a series of means. To say that an end is remote or distant, to say in fact that it is an end at all, is equivalent to saying that obstacles intervene between us and it. If, however, it remains a distant end, it becomes a *mere* end, that is a dream. As soon as we have projected it, we must begin to work backward in thought. We must change *what* is to be done into a *how,* the means whereby. The end thus reappears as a series of "what nexts," and the what next of chief importance is the one nearest the present state of the one acting. Only as the end is converted into means is it definitely conceived, or intellectually defined, to say nothing of being executable. Just as end, it is vague, cloudy, impressionistic. We do not *know* what we are really after until a *course* of action is mentally worked out. Aladdin with his lamp could dispense with translating ends into means, but no one else can do so.

Now the thing which is closest to us, the means within our power, is a habit. Some habit impeded by circumstances is the source of the projection of the end. It is also the primary means in its realization. The habit is propulsive and moves anyway toward some end, or result, whether it is projected as an end-in-view or not. The man who can walk does walk; the man who can talk does converse—if only with himself. How is this statement to be reconciled with the fact that we are not always walking and talking; that our habits seem so often to be latent, inoperative? Such inactivity holds only of *overt*, visibly obvious operation. In actuality each habit operates all the time of waking life; though like a member of a crew taking his turn at the wheel, its operation becomes the dominantly characteristic trait of an act only occasionally or rarely.

■■

Interpretive Questions

1. Why does Dewey think we can't have a clear idea of how to do things until we've already done them?

2. Why does Dewey think our goals are determined by our habits?

3. Why must a flanking movement be set up to break a bad habit or form a good one?

4. Why does Dewey say "the first or earliest means is the most important *end* to discover"? P. 24

5. If only a person who has good habits can know what the good is, can a person with bad habits ever become good?

III

What a Story Is

A famous writer once claimed that a novel should
"hold a mirror up to the high road," catching and
reflecting the passing scene just as it occurs. But
even the most realistic fiction does something
more interesting than this. Although a story may
tell us a great deal about life at a given time and
place, it is before all else a personal interpretation
of experience. Thoughtful writers do not merely
copy or imitate life, they shape it and endow it
with meaning. As we read a story, we experience
the world ordered by a particular intelligence and
filtered through a particular sensibility. We see

through the author's eyes. If we lend ourselves to the story fully, if we are seriously attentive, open, and alert, it may forever alter our own vision.

The best stories generally balance conflicting claims or points of view. As in life, situations in fiction are complex. Characters who are at odds with one another may both be right—or more likely, there will be right and wrong on both sides. Thoughtful stories present characters in the round, showing us more than we would know if we were in the story ourselves and more than we usually understand about the lives of those around us. By thinking about such stories, we come to see how each person has a distinct point of view—his or her own needs, desires, sorrows, and reasons for acting. We learn to look, in a conflict of interests, for the whole picture. Reading fiction not only broadens our sympathies for others but challenges us to re-examine ourselves, to move beyond our usual habits of perception and judgment.

Good stories require us to reach out to the author through active reading. As we read, it's important to ask ourselves what the author is trying to convey. What does he want us to think and feel? Why is he telling us this story? How does he feel about these characters? Does one character perhaps speak for the author?

Ultimately, readers must rely on their own responses to a story. A story then becomes a joint creation of the reader and the writer, a joint effort to make sense of life: a shared world created through words, to be imagined, explored, and interpreted. ▮▮

Happiness

Mary Lavin

Mother had a lot to say. This does not mean she was always talking but that we children felt the wells she drew upon were deep, deep, deep. Her theme was happiness: what it was, what it was not; where we might find it, where not; and how, if found, it must be guarded. Never must we confound it with pleasure. Nor think sorrow its exact opposite.

"Take Father Hugh," Mother's eyes flashed as she looked at him. "According to him, sorrow is an ingredient of happiness—a *necessary* ingredient, if you please!" And when he tried to protest she put up her hand. "There may be a freakish truth in the theory—for some people. But not for me. And not, I hope, for my children." She looked severely at us three girls. We laughed. None of us had had much experience with sorrow. Bea and I were children and Linda only a year old when our father died suddenly after a short illness that had not at first seemed serious. "I've known people to make sorrow a *substitute* for happiness," Mother said.

Father Hugh protested again. "You're not putting me in that class, I hope?"

Father Hugh, ever since our father died, had been the closest of anyone to us as a family, without being close to any one of us in particular—even to Mother. He lived in a monastery near our farm in County Meath, and he had been one of the celebrants at the Requiem High Mass our father's political importance had demanded. He met us that day for the first time, but he took to dropping in to see us, with the idea of filling the crater of loneliness left at our center. He did not know that there was a cavity in his own life, much less that we would fill it. He and Mother were both young in those days, and perhaps it gave scandal to some that he was so often in our house, staying till late into the night and, indeed, thinking nothing of stopping all night if there was any special reason, such as one of us being sick. He had even on occasion slept there if the night was too wet for tramping home across the fields.

When we girls were young, we were so used to having Father Hugh around that we never stood on ceremony with him but in his presence dried our hair and pared our nails and never minded what garments were strewn about. As for Mother—she thought nothing of running out of the bathroom in her slip, brushing her teeth or combing her hair, if she wanted to tell him something she might otherwise forget. And she brooked no criticism of her behavior. "Celibacy was never meant to take all the warmth and homeliness out of their lives," she said.

On this point, too, Bea was adamant. Bea, the middle sister, was our oracle. "I'm so glad he *has* Mother," she said, "as well as her having him, because it must be awful the way most women treat them—priests, I mean—as if they were pariahs. Mother treats him like a human being—that's all!"

And when it came to Mother's ears that there had been

gossip about her making free with Father Hugh, she opened
her eyes wide in astonishment. "But he's only a priest!" she
said.

Bea giggled. "It's a good job he didn't hear *that*," she said
to me afterwards. "It would undo the good she's done him.
You'd think he was a eunuch."

"Bea!" I said. "Do you think he's in love with her?"

"If so, he doesn't know it," Bea said firmly. "It's her soul
he's after! Maybe he wants to make sure of her in the next
world!"

But thoughts of the world to come never troubled Mother.
"If anything ever happens to me, children," she said, "suddenly, I mean, or when you are not near me, or I cannot speak to
you, I want you to promise you won't feel bad. There's no
need! Just remember that I had a happy life—and that if I had
to choose my kind of heaven I'd take it on this earth with you
again, no matter how much you might annoy me!"

You see, annoyance and fatigue, according to Mother, and
even illness and pain, could coexist with happiness. She had
a habit of asking people if they were happy at times and in
places that—to say the least of it—seemed to us inappropriate.
"But are you happy?" she'd probe as one lay sick and bathed
in sweat, or in the throes of a jumping toothache. And once
in our presence she made the inquiry of an old friend as he lay
upon his deathbed.

"Why not?" she said when we took her to task for it later.
"Isn't it more important than ever to be happy when you're
dying? Take my own father! You know what he said in his last
moments? On his deathbed, he defied me to name a man who
had enjoyed a better life. In spite of dreadful pain, his face
radiated happiness!" Mother nodded her head comfortably.
"Happiness drives out pain, as fire burns out fire."

Having no knowledge of our own to pit against hers, we
thirstily drank in her rhetoric. Only Bea was sceptical. "Per-

haps you *got* it from him, like spots, or fever," she said. "Or something that could at least be slipped from hand to hand."

"Do you think I'd have taken it if that were the case!" Mother cried. "Then, when he needed it most?"

"Not there and then!" Bea said stubbornly. "I meant as a sort of legacy."

"Don't you think in *that* case," Mother said, exasperated, "he would have felt obliged to leave it to your grandmother?"

Certainly we knew that in spite of his lavish heart our grandfather had failed to provide our grandmother with enduring happiness. He had passed that job on to Mother. And Mother had not made too good a fist of it, even when Father was living and she had him—and, later, us children—to help.

As for Father Hugh, he had given our grandmother up early in the game. "God Almighty couldn't make that woman happy," he said one day, seeing Mother's face, drawn and pale with fatigue, preparing for the nightly run over to her own mother's flat that would exhaust her utterly.

There were evenings after she came home from the library where she worked when we saw her stand with the car keys in her hand, trying to think which would be worse—to slog over there on foot, or take out the car again. And yet the distance was short. It was Mother's day that had been too long.

"Weren't you over to see her this morning?" Father Hugh demanded.

"No matter!" said Mother. She was no doubt thinking of the forlorn face our grandmother always put on when she was leaving. ("Don't say good night, Vera," Grandmother would plead. "It makes me feel too lonely. And you never can tell—you might slip over again before you go to bed!")

"Do you know the time?" Bea would say impatiently, if she happened to be with Mother. Not indeed that the lateness of the hour counted for anything, because in all likelihood Mother *would* go back, if only to pass by under the window and see that the lights were out, or stand and listen and make sure that as far as she could tell all was well.

"I wouldn't mind if she was happy," Mother said.

"And how do you know she's not?" we'd ask.

"When people are happy, I can feel it. Can't you?"

We were not sure. Most people thought our grandmother was a gay creature, a small birdy being who even at a great age laughed like a girl, and—more remarkably—sang like one, as she went about her day. But beak and claw were of steel. She'd think nothing of sending Mother back to a shop three times if her errands were not exactly right. "Not sugar like that— that's *too* fine; it's not castor sugar I want. But *not* as coarse as *that,* either. I want an in-between kind."

Provoked one day, my youngest sister, Linda, turned and gave battle. "You're mean!" she cried. "You love ordering people about!"

Grandmother preened, as if Linda had acclaimed an attribute. "I was always hard to please," she said. "As a girl, I used to be called Miss Imperious."

And Miss Imperious she remained as long as she lived, even when she was a great age. Her orders were then given a wry twist by the fact that as she advanced in age she took to calling her daughter Mother, as we did.

There was one great phrase with which our grandmother opened every sentence: "if only." "If only," she'd say, when we came to visit her—"if only you'd come earlier, before I was worn out expecting you!" Or if we were early, then if only it was later, after she'd had a rest and could enjoy us, be *able* for us. And if we brought her flowers, she'd sigh to think that if only we'd brought them the previous day she'd have had a visitor to appreciate them, or say it was a pity the stems weren't longer. If only we'd picked a few green leaves, or included some buds, because, she said disparagingly, the poor flowers we'd brought were already wilting. We might just as well not have brought them! As the years went on, Grandmother had a new bead to add to her rosary: if only her friends were not all dead! By their absence, they reduced to nil all *real* enjoyment in anything. Our own father—her son-in-law—was the one person who had ever gone close to pleasing her. But even here there had been a snag. "If only he was my real son!" she used to say, with a sigh.

Mother's mother lived on through our childhood and into our early maturity (though she outlived the money our grandfather left her), and in our minds she was a complicated mixture of valiance and defeat. Courageous and generous within the limits of her own life, her simplest demand was yet enormous in the larger frame of Mother's life, and so we never could see her with the same clarity of vision with which we saw our grandfather, or our own father. Them we saw only through Mother's eyes.

"Take your grandfather!" she'd cry, and instantly we'd see him, his eyes burning upon us—yes, upon *us*, although in his day only one of us had been born: me. At another time, Mother would cry, "Take your own father!" and instantly we'd see *him* —tall, handsome, young, and much more suited to marry one of us than poor bedraggled Mother.

Most fascinating of all were the times Mother would say "Take me!" By magic then, staring down the years, we'd see blazingly clear a small girl with black hair and buttoned boots, who, though plain and pouting, burned bright, like a star. "I was happy, you see," Mother said. And we'd strain hard to try and understand the mystery of the light that still radiated from her. "I used to lean along a tree that grew out over the river," she said, "and look down through the gray leaves at the water flowing past below, and I used to think it was not the stream that flowed but me, spread-eagled over it, who flew through the air! Like a bird! That I'd found the secret!" She made it seem there might *be* such a secret, just waiting to be found.

Another time she'd dream that she'd be a great singer.

"We didn't know you sang, Mother!"

She had to laugh. "Like a crow," she said.

Sometimes she used to think she'd swim the Channel.

"Did you swim *that* well, Mother?"

"Oh, not really—just the breaststroke," she said. "And then only by the aid of two pig bladders blown up by my father and tied around my middle. But I used to throb—yes, throb—with happiness."

Behind Mother's back, Bea raised her eyebrows.

What was it, we used to ask ourselves—that quality that she, we felt sure, misnamed? Was it courage? Was it strength, health, or high spirits? Something you could not give or take—a conundrum? A game of catch-as-catch-can?

"I know," cried Bea. "A sham!"

Whatever it was, we knew that Mother would let no wind of violence from within or without tear it from her. Although, one evening when Father Hugh was with us, our astonished ears heard her proclaim that there might be a time when one had to slacken hold on it—let go—to catch at it again with a surer hand. In the way, we supposed, that the high-wire walker up among the painted stars of his canvas sky must wait to fling himself through the air until the bar he catches at has started to sway perversely from him. Oh no, no! That downward drag at our innards we could not bear, the belly swelling to the shape of a pear. Let happiness go by the board. "After all, lots of people seem to make out without it," Bea cried. It was too tricky a business. And might it not be that one had to be born with a flair for it?

"A flair would not be enough," Mother answered. "Take Father Hugh. He, if anyone, had a flair for it—a natural capacity! You've only to look at him when he's off guard, with you children, or helping me in the garden. But he rejects happiness! He casts it from him."

"That is simply not true, Vera," cried Father Hugh, over-hearing her. "It's just that I don't place an inordinate value on it like you. I don't think it's enough to carry one all the way. To the end, I mean—and after."

"Oh, don't talk about the end when we're only in the middle," cried Mother. And, indeed, at that moment her own face shone with such happiness it was hard to believe that her earth was not her heaven. Certainly it was her constant contention that of happiness she had had a lion's share. This, however, we, in private, doubted. Perhaps there were times when she had had a surplus of it—when she was young, say, with her redoubtable father, whose love blazed circles around her, making winter into summer and ice into fire. Perhaps she did have a brimming measure in her early married years. By straining hard, we could find traces left in our minds from those days of milk and honey. Our father, while he lived, had cast a magic over everything, for us as well as for her. He held his love up over us like an umbrella and kept off the troubles that afterwards came down on us, pouring cats and dogs!

But if she did have more than the common lot of happiness in those early days, what use was that when we could remember so clearly how our father's death had ravaged her? And how could we forget the distress it brought on us when, afraid to let her out of our sight, Bea and I stumbled after her everywhere, through the woods and along the bank of the river, where, in the weeks that followed, she tried vainly to find peace.

The summer after Father died, we were invited to France to stay with friends, and when she went walking on the cliffs at Fécamp our fears for her grew frenzied, so that we hung on to her arm and dragged at her skirt, hoping that like leaded weights we'd pin her down if she went too near to the edge. But at night we had to abandon our watch, being forced to follow the conventions of a family still whole—a home still intact—and go to bed at the same time as the other children. It was at that hour, when the coast guard was gone from his rowing boat offshore and the sand was as cold and gray as the sea, that Mother liked to swim. And when she had washed, kissed, and left us, our hearts almost died inside us and we'd creep out of bed again to stand in our bare feet at the mansard and watch as she ran down the shingle, striking out when she reached the water where, far out, wave and sky and mist were one, and the grayness closed over her. If we took our eyes off her for an instant, it was impossible to find her again.

"Oh, make her turn back, God, please!" I prayed out loud one night.

Startled, Bea turned away from the window. "She'll *have* to turn back sometime, won't she? Unless . . . ?"

Locking our damp hands together, we stared out again. "She wouldn't!" I whispered. "It would be a sin!"

Secure in the deterring power of sin, we let out our breath. Then Bea's breath caught again. "What if she went out so far she used up all her strength? She couldn't swim back! It wouldn't be a sin then!"

"It's the intention that counts," I whispered.

A second later, we could see an arm lift heavily up and wearily cleave down, and at last Mother was in the shallows, wading back to shore.

"Don't let her see us!" cried Bea. As if our chattering teeth would not give us away when she looked in at us before she went to her own room on the other side of the corridor, where, later in the night, sometimes the sound of crying would reach us.

What was it worth—a happiness bought that dearly.

Mother had never questioned it. And once she told us, "On a wintry day, I brought my own mother a snowdrop. It was the first one of the year—a bleak bud that had come up stunted before its time—and I meant it for a sign. But do you know what your grandmother said? 'What good are snowdrops to me now?' Such a thing to say! What good is a snowdrop at all if it doesn't hold its value always, and never lose it! Isn't that the whole point of a snowdrop? And that is the whole point of happiness, too! What good would it be if it could be erased without trace? Take me and those daffodils!" Stooping, she buried her face in a bunch that lay on the table waiting to be put in vases. "If they didn't hold their beauty absolute and inviolable, do you think I could bear the sight of them after what happened when your father was in hospital?"

It was a fair question. When Father went to hospital, Mother went with him and stayed in a small hotel across the street so she could be with him all day from early to late. "Because it was so awful for him—being in Dublin!" she said. "You have no idea how he hated it."

That he was dying neither of them realized. How could they know, as it rushed through the sky, that their star was a falling star! But one evening when she'd left him asleep Mother came home for a few hours to see how we were faring, and it broke her heart to see the daffodils out all over the place—in the woods, under the trees, and along the sides of the avenue. There had never been so many, and she thought how awful it was that Father was missing them. "You sent up little bunches to him, you poor dears!" she said. "Sweet little bunches, too—squeezed tight as posies by your little fists! But stuffed into vases they couldn't really make up to him for not being able to see them growing!"

So on the way back to the hospital she stopped her car and pulled a great bunch—the full of her arms. "They took up the whole back seat," she said, "and I was so excited at the thought of walking into his room and dumping them on his bed—you know—just plomping them down so he could smell them, and feel them, and look and look! I didn't mean them to be put in vases, or anything ridiculous like that—it would have taken a rainwater barrel to hold them. Why, I could hardly see over them as I came up the steps; I kept tripping. But when I came into the hall, that nun—I told you about her—that nun came up to me, sprang out of nowhere it seemed, although I know now that she was waiting for me, knowing that somebody had to bring me to my senses. But the way she did it! Reached out and grabbed the flowers, letting lots of them fall—I remember them getting stood on. "Where are you going with those foolish flowers, you foolish woman?" she said. "Don't you know your husband is dying? Your prayers are all you can give him now!"

"She was right. I *was* foolish. But I wasn't cured. Afterwards, it was nothing but foolishness the way I dragged you children after me all over Europe. As if any one place was going to be different from another, any better, any less desolate. But there was great satisfaction in bringing you places your father and I had planned to bring you—although in fairness to him I must say that he would not perhaps have brought you so young. And he would not have had an ulterior motive. But above all, he would not have attempted those trips in such a dilapidated car."

Oh, that car! It was a battered and dilapidated red sports car, so depleted of accessories that when, eventually, we got a new car Mother still stuck out her hand on bends, and in wet weather jumped out to wipe the windscreen with her sleeve. And if fussed, she'd let down the window and shout at people, forgetting she now had a horn. How we had ever fitted into it with all our luggage was a miracle.

"You were never lumpish—any of you!" Mother said proudly. "But you were very healthy and very strong." She turned to me. "Think of how you got that car up the hill in Switzerland!"

"The Alps are not hills, Mother!" I pointed out coldly, as

I had done at the time, when, as actually happened, the car failed to make it on one of the inclines. Mother let it run back until it wedged against the rock face, and I had to get out and push till she got going again in first gear. But when it got started it couldn't be stopped to pick me up until it got to the top, where they had to wait for me, and for a very long time.

"Ah, well," she said, sighing wistfully at the thought of those trips. "You got something out of them, I hope. All that traveling must have helped you with your geography and your history."

We looked at each other and smiled, and then Mother herself laughed. "Remember the time," she said, "when we were in Italy, and it was Easter, and all the shops were chock-full of food? The butchers' shops had poultry and game hanging up outside the doors, fully feathered, and with their poor heads dripping blood, and in the windows they had poor little lambs and suckling pigs and young goats, all skinned and hanging by their hind feet." Mother shuddered. "They think so much about food. I found it revolting. I had to hurry past. But Linda, who must have been only four then, dragged at me and stared and stared. You know how children are at that age; they have a morbid fascination for what is cruel and bloody. Her face was flushed and her eyes were wide. I hurried her back to the hotel. But next morning she crept into my room. She crept up to me and pressed against me. 'Can't we go back, just once, and look again at that shop?' she whispered. 'The shop where they have the little children hanging up for Easter!' It was the young goats, of course, but I'd said 'kids,' I suppose. How we laughed." But her face was grave. "You were *so* good on those trips, all of you," she said. "You were really very good children in general. Otherwise I would never have put so much effort into rearing you, because I wasn't a bit maternal. You brought out the best in me! I put an unnatural effort into you, of course, because I was taking my standards from your father, forgetting that his might not have remained so inflexible if he had lived to middle age and was beset by life, like other parents."

"Well, the job is nearly over now, Vera," said Father Hugh. "And you didn't do so badly."

"That's right, Hugh," said Mother, and she straightened up, and put her hand to her back the way she sometimes did in the garden when she got up from her knees after weeding. "I didn't go over to the enemy anyway! We survived!" Then a flash of defiance came into her eyes. "And we were happy. That's the main thing!"

Father Hugh frowned. "There you go again!" he said.

Mother turned on him. "I don't think you realize the onslaughts that were made upon our happiness! The minute Robert died, they came down on me—cohorts of relatives, friends, even strangers, all draped in black, opening their arms like bats to let me pass into their company. 'Life is a vale of tears,' they said. 'You are privileged to find it out so young!' Ugh! After I staggered onto my feet and began to take hold of life once more, they fell back defeated. And the first day I gave a laugh—pouff, they were blown out like candles. They weren't living in a real world at all; they belonged to a ghostly world where life was easy: all one had to do was sit and weep. It takes effort to push back the stone from the mouth of the tomb and walk out."

Effort. Effort. Ah, but that strange-sounding word could invoke little sympathy from those who had not learned yet what it meant. Life must have been hardest for Mother in those years when we older ones were at college—no longer children, and still dependent on her. Indeed, we made more demands on her than ever then, having moved into new areas of activity and emotion. And our friends! Our friends came and went as freely as we did ourselves, so that the house was often like a café—and one where pets were not prohibited but took their places on our chairs and beds, as regardless as the people.

And anyway it was hard to have sympathy for someone who got things into such a state as Mother. All over the house there was clutter. Her study was like the returned-letter department of a post office, with stacks of paper everywhere, bills paid and unpaid, letters answered and unanswered, tax returns, pamphlets, leaflets. If by mistake we left the door open on a windy day, we came back to find papers flapping through the air like frightened birds. Efficient only in that she managed eventually to conclude every task she began, it never seemed possible to outsiders that by Mother's methods anything whatever could be accomplished. In an attempt to keep order elsewhere, she made her own room the clearinghouse into which the rest of us put everything: things to be given away, things to be mended, things to be stored, things to be treasured, things to be returned—even things to be thrown out! By the end of the year, the room resembled an obsolescence dump. And no one could help her; the chaos of her life was as personal as an act of creation—one might as well try to finish another person's poem.

As the years passed, Mother rushed around more hectically. And although Bea and I had married and were not at home anymore, except at holiday time and for occasional weekends, Linda was noisier than the two of us put together had been, and for every follower we had brought home she brought twenty. The house was never still. Now that we were reduced to being visitors, we watched Mother's tension mount to vertigo, knowing that, like a spinning top, she could not rest till she fell. But now at the smallest pretext Father Hugh would call in the doctor and Mother would be put on the mail boat and dispatched for London. For it was essential that she get far enough away to make phoning home every night prohibitively costly.

Unfortunately, the thought of departure often drove a spur into her and she redoubled her effort to achieve order in her affairs. She would be up until the early hours ransacking her desk. To her, as always, the shortest parting entailed a preparation as for death. And as if it were her end that was at hand, we would all be summoned, although she had no time to speak a word to us, because five minutes before departure she would still be attempting to reply to letters that were the acquisition of weeks and would have taken whole days to dispatch.

"Don't you know the taxi is at the door, Vera?" Father Hugh would say, running his hand through his gray hair and looking very disheveled himself. She had him at times as distracted as herself. "You can't do any more. You'll have to leave the rest till you come back."

"I can't, I can't!" Mother would cry. "I'll have to cancel my plans."

One day, Father Hugh opened the lid of her case, which was strapped up in the hall, and with a swipe of his arm he cleared all the papers on the top of the desk pell-mell into the suitcase. "You can sort them on the boat," he said, "or the train to London!"

Thereafter, Mother's luggage always included an empty case to hold the unfinished papers on her desk. And years afterwards a steward on the Irish Mail told us she was a familiar figure, working away at letters and bills nearly all the way from Holyhead to Euston. "She gave it up about Rugby or Crewe," he said. "She'd get talking to someone in the compartment." He smiled. "There was one time coming down the train I was just in time to see her close up the window with a guilty look. I didn't say anything, but I think she'd emptied those papers of hers out the window!"

Quite likely. When we were children, even a few hours away from us gave her composure. And in two weeks or less, when she'd come home, the well of her spirit would be freshened. We'd hardly know her—her step so light, her eye so bright, and her love and patience once more freely flowing. But in no time at all the house would fill up once more with the noise and confusion of too many people and too many animals, and again we'd be fighting our corner with cats and dogs, bats, mice, bees, and even wasps. "Don't kill it!" Mother would cry if we raised a hand to an angry wasp. "Just catch it, dear, and put it outside. Open the window and let it fly away!" But even this treatment could at times be deemed too harsh. "Wait a minute. Close the window!" she'd cry. "It's too cold outside. It will die. That's why it came in, I suppose! Oh dear, what will we do?" Life would be going full blast again.

There was only one place Mother found rest. When she was at breaking point and fit to fall, she'd go out into the garden—not to sit or stroll around but to dig, to drag up weeds, to move great clumps of corms or rhizomes, or indeed quite frequently to haul huge rocks from one place to another. She was always laying down a path, building a dry wall, or making compost heaps as high as hills. However jaded she might be going out, when dark forced her in at last her step had the spring of a daisy. So if she did not succeed in defining happiness to our understanding, we could see that whatever it was, she possessed it to the full when she was in her garden.

One of us said as much one Sunday when Bea and I had dropped round for the afternoon. Father Hugh was with us again. "It's an unthinking happiness, though," he caviled. We were standing at the drawing room window, looking out to where in the fading light we could see Mother on her knees weeding, in the long border that stretched from the house right down to the woods. "I wonder how she'd take it if she were stricken down and had to give up that heavy work!" he said. Was he perhaps a little jealous of how she could stoop and bend? He himself had begun to use a stick. I was often a little jealous of her myself, because although I was married and had children of my own, I had married young and felt the weight of living as heavy as a weight of years. "She doesn't take enough care of herself," Father Hugh said sadly. "Look at her out there with nothing under her knees to protect her from the damp ground." It was almost too dim for us to see her, but even in the drawing room it was chilly. "She should not be let stay out there after the sun goes down."

"Just you try to get her in then!" said Linda, who had come into the room in time to hear him. "Don't you know by now anyway that what would kill another person only seems to make Mother thrive?"

Father Hugh shook his head again. "You seem to forget it's not younger she's getting!" He fidgeted and fussed, and several times went to the window to stare out apprehensively. He was really getting quite elderly.

"Come and sit down, Father Hugh," Bea said, and to take his mind off Mother she turned on the light and blotted out the garden. Instead of seeing through the window, we saw into it as into a mirror, and there between the flower-laden tables and the lamps it was ourselves we saw moving vaguely. Like Father Hugh, we, too, were waiting for her to come in before we called an end to the day.

"Oh, this is ridiculous!" Father Hugh cried at last. "She'll have to listen to reason." And going back to the window he threw it open. "Vera!" he called. "Vera!"—sternly, so sternly that, more intimate than an endearment, his tone shocked us. "She didn't hear me," he said, turning back blinking at us in the lighted room. "I'm going out to get her." And in a minute he was gone from the room. As he ran down the garden path, we stared at each other, astonished; his step, like his voice, was the step of a lover. "I'm coming, Vera!" he cried.

Although she was never stubborn except in things that mattered, Mother had not moved. In the wholehearted way she did everything, she was bent down close to the ground. It wasn't the light only that was dimming; her eyesight also was failing, I thought, as instinctively I followed Father Hugh.

But halfway down the path I stopped. I had seen something he had not: Mother's hand that appeared to support itself in a forked branch of an old tree peony she had planted as a bride was not in fact gripping it but impaled upon it. And the hand that appeared to be grubbing in the clay in fact was sunk into the soft mold. "Mother!" I screamed, and I ran forward, but when I reached her I covered my face with my hands. "Oh Father Hugh!" I cried. "Is she dead?"

It was Bea who answered, hysterical. "She is! She is!" she cried, and she began to pound Father Hugh on the back with her fists, as if his pessimistic words had made this happen.

But Mother was not dead. And at first the doctor even offered hope of her pulling through. But from the moment Father Hugh lifted her up to carry her into the house we ourselves had no hope, seeing how effortlessly he, who was not strong, could carry her. When he put her down on her bed, her head hardly creased the pillow. Mother lived for four more hours.

Like the days of her life, those four hours that Mother lived were packed tight with concern and anxiety. Partly conscious, partly delirious, she seemed to think the counterpane was her desk, and she scrabbled her fingers upon it as if trying to sort out a muddle of bills and correspondence. No longer indifferent now, we listened, anguished, to the distracted cries that had for all our lifetime been so familiar to us. "Oh, where is it? Where is it? I had it a minute ago! Where on earth did I put it?"

"Vera, Vera, stop worrying," Father Hugh pleaded, but she waved him away and went on sifting through the sheets as if they were sheets of paper. "Oh, Vera!" he begged. "Listen to me. Do you not know—"

Bea pushed between them. "You're not to tell her!" she commanded. "Why frighten her?"

"But it ought not to frighten her," said Father Hugh. "This

is what I was always afraid would happen—that she'd be frightened when it came to the end."

At that moment, as if to vindicate him, Mother's hands fell idle on the coverlet, palm upward and empty. And turning her head she stared at each of us in turn, beseechingly. "I cannot face it," she whispered. "I can't! I can't! I can't!"

"Oh, my God!" Bea said, and she started to cry.

"Vera. For God's sake listen to me," Father Hugh cried, and pressing his face to hers, as close as a kiss, he kept whispering to her, trying to cast into the dark tunnel before her the light of his own faith.

But it seemed to us that Mother must already be looking into God's exigent eyes. "I can't!" she cried. "I can't!"

Then her mind came back from the stark world of the spirit to the world where her body was still detained, but even that world was now a whirling kaleidoscope of things which only she could see. Suddenly her eyes focused, and, catching at Father Hugh, she pulled herself up a little and pointed to something we could not see. "They ought to be put in water anyway," she said, and, leaning over the edge of the bed, she pointed to the floor. "Don't step on that one!" she said sharply. Then, more sharply still, she addressed us all. "Have them sent to the ward," she said peremptorily. "Don't let that nun take them; she'll only put them on the altar. And God doesn't want them! He made them for *us*—not for Himself!"

It was the familiar rhetoric that all her life had characterized her utterances. For a moment we were mystified. Then Bea gasped. "The daffodils!" she cried. "The day Father died!" And over her face came the light that had so often blazed over Mother's. Leaning across the bed, she pushed Father Hugh aside. And, putting out her hands, she held Mother's face between her palms as tenderly as if it were the face of a child. "It's all right, Mother. You don't *have* to face it! It's over!"

Then she who had so fiercely forbade Father Hugh to do so blurted out the truth. "You've finished with this world, Mother," she said, and, confident that her tidings were joyous, her voice was strong.

Mother made the last effort of her life and grasped at Bea's meaning. She let out a sigh, and, closing her eyes, she sank back, and this time her head sank so deep into the pillow that it would have been dented had it been a pillow of stone.

Interpretive Questions

1. Why was Mother happy when she was doing the breaststroke, running back and forth to her mother's house after a long day's work, or hauling huge rocks in the garden?

2. Why does Bea, rather than the narrator, receive the legacy of happiness from Mother?

3. Why is Mother sure happiness can coexist with annoyance and fatigue, illness and pain, concern and anxiety?

4. What does Mother mean by saying that Father Hugh has a flair for happiness but rejects it?

5. By whispering "I cannot face it," does Mother vindicate Father Hugh's belief that she is not prepared for the end?

IV

By and About Plato

(427?–347 B.C.)

Plato was present in the courtroom when his teacher Socrates was convicted on false charges and condemned to death. In the *Apology,* his account of the trial, Plato presents Socrates' explanation of his way of life:

> I have never liked an ordinary quiet life. I did not care for the things that most people care about: making money, having a comfortable home, high military or civil rank, and all the other activities—political appointments, secret societies, party organizations—which go on in our city; I thought that I was really too strict in my principles to survive if I went in for this sort of thing. So instead of taking a course which would have done no good either to you or to me, I set myself to do you individually in private what I hold to be the greatest possible service: I tried to persuade each one of you not to think more of practical advantages than of his mental and moral well-being.

Socrates says that he does not fear the death sentence:

> To be afraid of death is only another form of thinking that one is wise when one is not; it is to think that one knows what one does not know. No one knows with regard to death whether it is really the greatest blessing that can happen to a man; but people dread it as though they were certain that it is the greatest evil. . . . If I were to claim to be wiser than my neightbor in any respect, it would be in this: that not possessing any real knowledge of what comes after death, I am also conscious that I do not possess it.

Plato followed his teacher's method of philosophizing through conversation and used the dialogue form in his written works. He never gives himself a role in the dialogues, but often he expresses his point of view through Socrates or some other character. On good men becoming rulers, he has Socrates say:

> Good men are unwilling to rule, either for money's sake or for honor. They have no wish to be called mercenary for demanding to be paid, or thieves for makinng a secret profit from their office;

nor yet will honors tempt them, for they are not ambitious. So they must be forced to consent to rule under threat of penalty; that may be why a readiness to accept power under no constraint is thought discreditable. And the heaviest penalty for declining to rule is to be ruled by some inferior to yourself. That is the fear, I believe, that makes decent people accept power.

Another character discusses Socrates' way of philosophizing:

Anyone listening to Socrates for the first time would find his arguments extremely laughable. . . . He talks about pack asses and blacksmiths and shoemakers and tanners, and he always seems to be saying the same old thing in just the same old way, so that anyone who wasn't used to his style and wasn't very quick on the uptake would naturally take it for the most utter nonsense. But if you open up his arguments, you'll find that they're the only arguments in the world that have any sense at all.

Socrates (469–399 B.C.) devoted himself to discussing the nature of the good life. He urged his fellow Athenians to live and act according to their rational convictions about virtue, piety, and justice, regardless of the opinions of others. "The unexamined life," he said, "is not worth living." His questioning of established beliefs brought Socrates into conflict with many in Athens: when he was nearing seventy, he was put on trial for religious heresy and for corrupting the youth of the city. Plato, his disciple, wrote accounts of the trial and of Socrates' actions before his execution. The Crito *tells of Socrates' refusal to escape when his old friend Crito offers to bribe the jailers. The dialogue begins as Socrates awakens in his cell with Crito sitting beside him.*

Crito

Plato

SOCRATES: Here already, Crito? Surely it is still early?

CRITO: Indeed it is.

SOCRATES: About what time?

CRITO: Just before dawn.

SOCRATES: I wonder that the warder paid any attention to you.

CRITO: He is used to me now, Socrates, because I come here so often; besides, he is under some small obligation to me.

SOCRATES: Have you only just come, or have you been here for long?

CRITO: Fairly long.

SOCRATES: Then why didn't you wake me at once, instead of sitting by my bed so quietly?

CRITO: I wouldn't dream of such a thing, Socrates. I only wish I were not so sleepless and depressed myself. I have been wondering at you, because I saw how comfortably you were

---

*A selection from *Crito*.

sleeping; and I deliberately didn't wake you because I wanted you to go on being as comfortable as you could. I have often felt before in the course of my life how fortunate you are in your disposition, but I feel it more than ever now in your present misfortune when I see how easily and placidly you put up with it.

SOCRATES: Well, really, Crito, it would be hardly suitable for a man of my age to resent having to die.

CRITO: Other people just as old as you are get involved in these misfortunes, Socrates, but their age doesn't keep them from resenting it when they find themselves in your position. . . .

. . . Look here, Socrates, it is still not too late to take my advice and escape. Your death means a double calamity for me. I shall not only lose a friend whom I can never possibly replace, but besides, a great many people who don't know you and me very well will be sure to think that I let you down, because I could have saved you if I had been willing to spend the money; and what could be more contemptible than to get a name for thinking more of money than of your friends? Most people will never believe that it was you who refused to leave this place although we tried our hardest to persuade you.

SOCRATES: But my dear Crito, why should we pay so much attention to what "most people" think? The really reasonable people, who have more claim to be considered, will believe that the facts are exactly as they are.

CRITO: You can see for yourself, Socrates, that one has to think of popular opinion as well. Your present position is quite enough to show that the capacity of ordinary people for causing trouble is not confined to petty annoyances, but has hardly any limits if you once get a bad name with them.

SOCRATES: I only wish that ordinary people *had* an unlimited capacity for doing harm; then they might have an unlimited power for doing good, which would be a splendid thing if it were so. Actually they have neither. They cannot make a man wise or stupid; they simply act at random. . . .

. . . Ought we to be guided and intimidated by the opinion of the many or by that of the one—assuming that there is someone with expert knowledge? Is it true that we ought to respect and fear this person more than all the rest put together; and that if we do not follow his guidance we shall spoil and mutilate that part of us which, as we used to say, is improved by right conduct and destroyed by wrong? Or is this all nonsense?

CRITO: No, I think it is true, Socrates. . . .

SOCRATES: . . . Our real duty, I fancy, since the argument leads that way, is to consider one question only . . . : Shall we be acting rightly in paying money and showing gratitude to these people who are going to rescue me, and in escaping or arranging the escape ourselves, or shall we really be acting wrongly in doing all this? If it becomes clear that such conduct is wrong, I cannot help thinking that the question whether we are sure to die, or to suffer any other ill effect for that matter, if we stand our ground and take no action, ought not to weigh with us at all in comparison with the risk of doing what is wrong.

CRITO: I agree with what you say, Socrates; but I wish you would consider what we ought to *do*. . . .

SOCRATES: Let us look at it together, my dear fellow; and if you can challenge any of my arguments, do so and I will listen to you; but if you can't, be a good fellow and stop telling me over and over again that I ought to leave this place without official permission. I am very anxious to obtain your approval before I adopt the course which I have in mind; I don't want to act against your convictions. Now give your attention to the starting point of this inquiry—I hope that you will be satisfied with my way of stating it—and try to answer my questions to the best of your judgment.

CRITO: Well, I will try.

SOCRATES: Do we say that one must never willingly do wrong, or does it depend upon circumstances? Is it true, as we have often agreed before, that there is no sense in which wrongdoing is good or honorable? Or have we jettisoned all our former convictions in these last few days? Can you and I at our age, Crito, have spent all these years in serious discussions without realizing that we were no better than a pair of children? Surely the truth is just what we have always said. Whatever the popular view is, and whether the alternative is pleasanter than the present one or even harder to bear, the fact remains that to do wrong is in every sense bad and dishonorable for the person who does it. Is that our view, or not?

CRITO: Yes, it is.

SOCRATES: Then in no circumstances must one do wrong.

CRITO: No.

SOCRATES: In that case one must not even do wrong when one is wronged, which most people regard as the natural course.

CRITO: Apparently not.

SOCRATES: Tell me another thing, Crito: ought one to do injuries or not?

CRITO: Surely not, Socrates.

SOCRATES: And tell me: is it right to do an injury in retaliation, as most people believe, or not?

CRITO: No, never.

SOCRATES: Because, I suppose, there is no difference between injuring people and wronging them.

CRITO: Exactly.

SOCRATES: So one ought not to return a wrong or an injury to any person, whatever the provocation is. Now be careful, Crito, that in making these single admissions you do not end by admitting something contrary to your real beliefs. I know that there are and always will be few people who think like this; and consequently between those who do think so and those who do not there can be no agreement on principle; they must always feel contempt when they observe one another's decisions. I want even you to consider very carefully whether you share my views and agree with me, and whether we can proceed with our discussion from the established hypothesis that it is never right to do a wrong or return a wrong or defend oneself against injury by retaliation; or whether you dissociate yourself from any share in this view as a basis for discussion. I have held it for a long time, and still hold it; but if you have formed any other opinion, say so and tell me what it is. If, on the other hand, you stand by what we have said, listen to my next point.

CRITO: Yes, I stand by it and agree with you. Go on.

SOCRATES: Well, here is my next point, or rather question. Ought one to fulfill all one's agreements, provided that they are right, or break them?

CRITO: One ought to fulfill them.

SOCRATES: Then consider the logical consequence. If we leave this place without first persuading the State to let us go, are we or are we not doing an injury, and doing it in a quarter where it is least justifiable? Are we or are we not abiding by our just agreements?

CRITO: I can't answer your question, Socrates; I am not clear in my mind.

SOCRATES: Look at it in this way. Suppose that while we were preparing to run away from here (or however one should describe it) the Laws and Constitution of Athens were to come and confront us and ask this question: "Now, Socrates, what are you proposing to do? Can you deny that by this act which you are contemplating you intend, so far as you have the

power, to destroy us, the Laws, and the whole State as well?
Do you imagine that a city can continue to exist and not be
turned upside down, if the legal judgments which are pronounced in it have no force but are nullified and destroyed by
private persons?"—how shall we answer this question, Crito,
and others of the same kind? There is much that could be said,
especially by a professional advocate, to protest against the
invalidation of this law which enacts that judgments once
pronounced shall be binding. Shall we say: "Yes, I do intend
to destroy the laws, because the State wronged me by passing
a faulty judgment at my trial"? Is this to be our answer, or
what?

CRITO: What you have just said, by all means, Socrates.

SOCRATES: Then what supposing the Laws say: "Was there
provision for this in the agreement between you and us, Socrates? Or did you undertake to abide by whatever judgments the
State pronounced?" If we expressed surprise at such language,
they would probably say: "Never mind our language, Socrates,
but answer our questions; after all, you are accustomed to the
method of question and answer. Come now, what charge do
you bring against us and the State, that you are trying to
destroy us? Did we not give you life in the first place? was it
not through us that your father married your mother and begot
you? Tell us, have you any complaint against those of us Laws
that deal with marriage?" "No, none," I should say. "Well,
have you any against the laws which deal with children's up-
bringing and education, such as you had yourself? Are you not
grateful to those of us Laws which were instituted for this end,
for requiring your father to give you a cultural and physical
education?" "Yes," I should say. "Very good. Then since you
have been born and brought up and educated, can you deny,
in the first place, that you were our child and servant, both you
and your ancestors? And if this is so, do you imagine that what

is right for us is equally right for you, and that whatever we try to do to you, you are justified in retaliating? You did not have equality of rights with your father, or your employer (supposing that you had one), to enable you to retaliate; you were not allowed to answer back when you were scolded or to hit back when you were beaten, or to do a great many other things of the same kind. Do you expect to have such license against your country and its laws that if we try to put you to death in the belief that it is right to do so, you on your part will try your hardest to destroy your country and us its Laws in return? and will you, the true devotee of goodness, claim that you are justified in doing so? Are you so wise as to have forgotten that compared with your mother and father and all the rest of your ancestors, your country is something far more precious, more venerable, more sacred, and held in greater honor both among gods and among all reasonable men? Do you not realize that you are even more bound to respect and placate the anger of your country than your father's anger? that if you cannot persuade your country you must do whatever it orders, and patiently submit to any punishment that it imposes, whether it be flogging or imprisonment? And if it leads you out to war, to be wounded or killed, you must comply, and it is right that you should do so; you must not give way or retreat or abandon your position. Both in war and in the lawcourts and everywhere else you must do whatever your city and your country commands, or else persuade it in accordance with universal justice; but violence is a sin even against your parents, and it is a far greater sin against your country."—What shall we say to this, Crito?—that what the Laws say is true, or not?

CRITO: Yes, I think so. *agrees*

SOCRATES: "Consider, then, Socrates," the Laws would probably continue, "whether it is also true for us to say that what you are now trying to do to us is not right. Although we have brought you into the world and reared you and educated you, and given you and all your fellow citizens a share in all the good things at our disposal, nevertheless by the very fact of granting our permission we openly proclaim this principle: that any Athenian, on attaining to manhood and seeing for himself the political organization of the state and us its Laws, is permitted, if he is not satisfied with us, to take his property and go away wherever he likes. If any of you chooses to go to one of our colonies, supposing that he should not be satisfied with us and the State, or to emigrate to any other country, not one of us Laws hinders or prevents him from going away wherever he likes, without any loss of property. On the other hand, if any one of you stands his ground when he can see how we administer justice and the rest of our public organization, we hold that by so doing he has in fact undertaken to do anything that we tell him; and we maintain that anyone who disobeys is guilty of doing wrong on three separate counts: first because we are his parents; and secondly because we are his guardians; and thirdly because, after promising obedience, he is neither obeying us nor persuading us to change our decision if we are at fault in any way; and although all our orders are in the form of proposals, not of savage commands, and we give him the choice of either persuading us or doing what we say, he is actually doing neither. These are the charges, Socrates, to which we say that you will be liable if you do what you are contemplating; and you will not be the least culpable of your fellow countrymen, but one of the most guilty." If I said, "Why do you say that?" they would no doubt pounce upon me with perfect justice and point out that there are very few people in Athens who have entered into this agreement with them as explicitly as I have. They would say: "Socrates, we have substantial evidence that you are satisfied with us and with the State. You would not have been so exceptionally reluctant to cross the borders of your country if you had not been exceptionally attached to it. You have never left the city to attend a festival or for any other purpose, except on some military expedition; you have never traveled abroad as other people do, and you have never felt the impulse to acquaint yourself with another country or constitution; you have been content with us and with our city. You have definitely chosen us, and undertaken to observe us in all your activities as a citizen; and as the crowning proof that you are satisfied with our city, you have begotten children in it. Furthermore, even at the time of your trial you could have proposed the penalty of banishment, if you had chosen to do so; that is, you could have done then with the sanction of the State what you are now trying to do without it. But whereas at that time you made a noble show of indifference if you had to die, and in fact preferred death, as you said, to banishment, now you show no respect for your earlier professions, and no regard for us, the Laws, whom you are trying to destroy; you are behaving like the lowest type of menial, trying to run away in spite of the contracts and undertakings by which you agreed to live as a member of our State. Now first answer this question: Are we or are we not speaking the truth when we say that you have undertaken, in deed if not in word, to live your life as a citizen in obedience to us?" What are we to say to that, Crito? Are we not bound to admit it?

CRITO: We cannot help it, Socrates.

SOCRATES: "It is a fact, then," they would say, "that you are breaking covenants and undertakings made with us, although you made them under no compulsion or misunderstanding and were not compelled to decide in a limited time; you had seventy years in which you could have left the country, if you were not satisfied with us or felt that the agreements were unfair. You did not choose Sparta or Crete—your favorite models of good government—or any other Greek or foreign

state; you could not have absented yourself from the city less
if you had been lame or blind or decrepit in some other way.
It is quite obvious that you stand by yourself above all other
Athenians in your affection for this city and for us its Laws—
who would care for a city without laws? And now, after all this,
are you not going to stand by your agreement? Yes, you are,
Socrates, if you will take our advice; and then you will at least
escape being laughed at for leaving the city.

"We invite you to consider what good you will do to yourself
or your friends if you commit this breach of faith and stain
your conscience. It is fairly obvious that the risk of being
banished and either losing their citizenship or having their
property confiscated will extend to your friends as well. As for
yourself, if you go to one of the neighboring states, such as
Thebes or Megara, which are both well governed, you will
enter them as an enemy to their constitution, and all good
patriots will eye you with suspicion as a destroyer of law and
order. Incidentally you will confirm the opinion of the jurors
who tried you that they gave a correct verdict; a destroyer of
laws might very well be supposed to have a destructive influence
upon young and foolish human beings. Do you intend, then,
to avoid well governed states and the higher forms of human
society? and if you do, will life be worth living? Or will you
approach these people and have the impudence to converse
with them? What arguments will you use, Socrates? The same
which you used here, that goodness and integrity, institutions
and laws, are the most precious possessions of mankind? Do
you not think that Socrates and everything about him will
appear in a disreputable light? You certainly ought to think so.
But perhaps you will retire from this part of the world and go
to Crito's friends in Thessaly? That is the home of indiscipline
and laxity, and no doubt they would enjoy hearing the amusing
story of how you managed to run away from prison by arraying

yourself in some costume or putting on a shepherd's smock or some other conventional runaway's disguise and altering your personal appearance. And will no one comment on the fact that an old man of your age, probably with only a short time to live, should dare to cling so greedily to life, at the price of violating the most stringent laws? Perhaps not, if you avoid irritating anyone. Otherwise, Socrates, you will hear a good many humiliating comments. So you will live as the toady and slave of all the populace, literally 'roistering in Thessaly,' as though you had left this country for Thessaly to attend a banquet there; and where will your discussions about goodness and uprightness be then, we should like to know? But of course you want to live for your children's sake, so that you may be able to bring them up and educate them. Indeed! by first taking them off to Thessaly and making foreigners of them, so that they may have that additional enjoyment? Or if that is not your intention, supposing that they are brought up here with you still alive, will they be better cared for and educated without you, because of course your friends will look after them? Will they look after your children if you go away to Thessaly, and not if you go away to the next world? Surely if those who profess to be your friends are worth anything, you must believe that they would care for them.

"No, Socrates; be advised by us your guardians, and do not think more of your children or of your life or of anything else than you think of what is right; so that when you enter the next world you may have all this to plead in your defense before the authorities there. It seems clear that if you do this thing, neither you nor any of your friends will be the better for it or be more upright or have a cleaner conscience here in this world, nor will it be better for you when you reach the next. As it is, you will leave this place, when you do, as the victim of a wrong done not by us, the Laws, but by your fellowmen.

But if you leave in that dishonorable way, returning wrong for wrong and evil for evil, breaking your agreements and covenants with us, and injuring those whom you least ought to injure—yourself, your friends, your country, and us—then you will have to face our anger in your lifetime, and in that place beyond when the laws of the other world know that you have tried, so far as you could, to destroy even us their brothers, they will not receive you with a kindly welcome. Do not take Crito's advice, but follow ours."

That, my dear friend Crito, I do assure you, is what I seem to hear them saying, just as a mystic seems to hear the strains of music; and the sound of their arguments rings so loudly in my head that I cannot hear the other side. I warn you that, as my opinion stands at present, it will be useless to urge a different view. However, if you think that you will do any good by it, say what you like.

CRITO: No, Socrates, I have nothing to say.

SOCRATES: Then give it up, Crito, and let us follow this course, since God points out the way.

Interpretive Questions

LAST PARAGRAPH

p. 59

1. Why does Socrates say that a single violation of a law represents an intent to destroy the Laws and the whole State?

   p. 64 TOP PARAGRAPH

2. Does Socrates think we should obey unjust laws if we cannot persuade the State to change them?

3. Does Socrates talk with Crito to obtain his approval or to discover the proper course of action?

4. Why does Socrates think he has made an agreement with the Laws rather than with his fellow citizens?

5. Why does Socrates regard citizens as servants of the Laws, rather than the Laws as servants of citizens?

Preparing for Discussion

The Great Books program is based on shared inquiry—the gradual unfolding of meaning that occurs when readers explore a story or essay in discussion. Shared inquiry cannot take place unless all participants have immersed themselves in the material and come to terms with it in their various individual ways. This kind of involvement teaches us to trust our own responses and to use them as the basis for interpretation.

Discussion should be a free exchange of ideas and a process of discovery. If you are seriously attentive to a good story or essay, you will come to discussion eager to share your ideas. During discussion you will feel less concern about being "right" or "wrong" than you will about increasing your understanding of the material itself.

As part of your preparation for discussion, read each selection at least twice, with a pen or pencil in hand, and make notes of your thoughts and feelings as you read. Your notes may take any form you like: underline a passage, put a question mark above a line, jot down a comment in the margin. If you are not allowed to mark your book, there are other ways to make notations: clip a note to an important page, use removable self-stick notes, or jot down your thoughts about a selection in a notebook reserved for the Great Books program. If you keep a special notebook, place a page number next to each note so that you can quickly refer to the passage on which the note is based.

On your first reading, make a note of what you don't understand, what seems important, and what you agree or disagree with. What you note, or the number of notes you make, doesn't matter; the very act of making notes will help you get involved with the material and begin thinking about it.

On a second reading you will find yourself making new notes, and probably more of them, simply because you have read the entire selection once before. New passages will strike you as important now that you know how the selection ends. You will discover connections between passages that you had missed on your first reading: the repetition of a significant word or phrase, a pattern of ideas or actions, or something in the beginning of a selection that prepares you for the ending. You may also begin to see how the different parts fit together and why the author uses certain phrases.

Having completed both readings, you should review your notes and try to turn some of them into questions that you would like the group's help in answering. It may be appropriate to raise these questions during discussion of the leader's questions, or the leader may set aside a separate time for them.

The following example shows how one student took notes on the *Crito*.

SOCRATES: Look at it in this way. Suppose that while we were preparing to run away from here (or however one should describe it), the Laws and Constitution of Athens were to come and confront us and ask this question: "Now, Socrates, what are you proposing to do? Can you deny that by this act which you are contemplating you intend, so far as you have the power, to destroy us, the Laws, and the whole State as well? Do you imagine that a city can continue to exist, and not be turned upside down, if the legal judgments which are pronounced in it have no force, but are nullified and destroyed by private persons?"—How shall we answer this question, Crito, and others of the same kind? There is much that could be said, especially by a professional advocate, to protest against the invalidation of this law which enacts that judgments once pronounced shall be binding. Shall we say: "Yes, I do intend to destroy the laws, because the State wronged me by passing a faulty judgment at my trial"? Is this to be our answer, or what?

[margin notes:]
Socrates personifies Laws and Constitution

Laws' accusation seems overstated

examples?

Why does Socrates agree so quickly?

If Socrates was unjustly condemned, why isn't escape ok?

V

Interpretation

Interpretation is the effort we make to understand what we read—to explain what an author's language is designed to make us think or feel. Interpreting the stories in this series requires effort because they have been written by keen thinkers. What these authors have to say cannot be taken in hastily. They use words carefully and precisely, but sometimes their language is difficult.

We begin to interpret a story the first time we read it. It is helpful to make notes on what we understand and what puzzles us during this reading. Reading slowly is also important. Whenever you don't understand a passage, try pausing and rereading it. If an unfamiliar word stops you, look it up in a dictionary. If the author has used an ordinary word in an unfamiliar way, try to figure out its meaning in the context of the words or sentences surrounding it. If the passage is still unclear, make a note of it and move on; the meaning may be clarified later in the selection.

By the end of your first reading you may have only a glimmer of the selection's meaning, but your bits and pieces of understanding will help you on a second reading. This time you will be able to think about the selection as a whole, not just about the next step in an argument or how a story will end. You will be in a better position to consider why an author made a particular statement, why it was phrased in a certain way, and why it appears where it does in the selection. You should at least be able to pinpoint why you don't understand what the author is saying. During this reading, make a note of connections you find between different parts of the selection. Check the meaning of what you think you understand by expressing it in your own words.

Discussion is the last step in the interpretive process. It is an opportunity to compare your understanding of a selection's meaning with the interpretations of others, to discover significant passages that you may have overlooked, and to hear explanations of what you didn't understand. Occasionally discussion may provide your first inkling about a selection's meaning, but more often it explores ideas you had while reading. ■▮

By and About John Stuart Mill

(1806–1873)

John Stuart Mill, the eldest son of the British philosopher James Mill, was subjected to a rigorous educational experiment designed by his father:

> Mine . . . was not an education of cram. My father never permitted anything which I learned to degenerate into a mere exercise of memory. He strove to make the understanding not only go along with every step of the teaching, but if possible, precede it. Anything which would be found out by thinking I was never told, until I had exhausted my efforts to find it out for myself. . . .

Mill was a fervent egalitarian in private and in public life. As a Member of Parliament, he took an active part in the debates preceding passage of the 1867 Reform Bill. With his motion that the word "man" be replaced by the word "person," the question of a woman's right to vote was raised in legislative assembly for the first time in modern history. In *The Subjection of Women*, Mill argues that freedom is as vital to women as it is to men:

> After the primary necessities of food and raiment, freedom is the first and strongest want of human nature. . . . Let any man call to mind what he himself felt on emerging from boyhood—from the tutelage and control of even loved and affectionate elders—and entering upon the responsibilities of manhood. Was it not like the physical effect of taking off a heavy weight, or releasing him from obstructive, even if not otherwise painful, bonds? Did he not feel twice as much alive, twice as much a human being, as before? And does he imagine that women have none of these feelings?

He foresees a new era based on the free association of equals:

> Already in modern life, and more and more as it progressively improves, command and obedience become exceptional facts in life, equal association its general rule. The morality of the first ages rested on the obligation to submit to power; that of the ages next following, on the right of the weak to the forbearance and

protection of the strong. How much longer is one form of society and life to content itself with the morality made for another? We have had the morality of submission, and the morality of chivalry and generosity; the time is now come for the morality of justice.

Of happiness, Mill writes:

I never, indeed, wavered in the conviction that happiness is the test of all rules of conduct, and the end of life. But I now thought that this end was only to be attained by not making it the direct end. Those only are happy (I thought) who have their minds fixed on some object other than their own happiness; on the happiness of others, on the improvement of mankind, even on some art or pursuit, followed not as a means, but as itself an ideal end. Aiming thus at something else, they find happiness by the way. . . . Ask yourself whether you are happy, and you cease to be so. The only chance is to treat, not happiness, but some end external to it, as the purpose of life. Let your self-consciousness, your scrutiny, your self-interrogation, exhaust themselves on that; and if otherwise fortunately circumstanced you will inhale happiness with the air you breathe, without dwelling on it or thinking about it, without either forestalling it in imagination, or putting it to flight by fatal questioning.

The individual's freedom within society is the subject of On Liberty. *Mill contends that the individual needs many different kinds of freedom—freedom of thought and feeling, freedom of expression, freedom of taste—to develop as a human being. The greatest threat to individual freedom, according to Mill, is the tyranny of the majority as exercised through public opinion. In our selection, Mill lays down the principle that should guide society in dealing with its adult members: Society may interfere with a person's freedom of action only if he or she is likely to harm others. Interference on the grounds that a person may harm himself or does not know what is best for himself is never justified.*

On Liberty

John Stuart Mill

The subject of this essay is not the so-called liberty of the will, so unfortunately opposed to the misnamed doctrine of philosophical necessity; but civil, or social liberty: the nature and limits of the power which can be legitimately exercised by society over the individual. A question seldom stated and hardly ever discussed in general terms, but which profoundly influences the practical controversies of the age by its latent presence, and is likely soon to make itself recognized as the vital question of the future. It is so far from being new, that, in a certain sense, it has divided mankind almost from the remotest ages; but in the stage of progress into which the more civilized portions of the species have now entered, it presents itself under new conditions, and requires a different and more fundamental treatment.

The struggle between liberty and authority is the most conspicuous feature in the portions of history with which we are

---

*A selection from *On Liberty*.

earliest familiar, particularly in that of Greece, Rome, and England. But in old times this contest was between subjects, or some classes of subjects, and the government. By liberty, was meant protection against the tyranny of the political rulers. The rulers were conceived (except in some of the popular governments of Greece) as in a necessarily antagonistic position to the people whom they ruled. They consisted of a governing One, or a governing tribe or caste, who derived their authority from inheritance or conquest, who, at all events, did not hold it at the pleasure of the governed, and whose supremacy men did not venture, perhaps did not desire, to contest, whatever precautions might be taken against its oppressive exercise. Their power was regarded as necessary, but also as highly dangerous; as a weapon which they would attempt to use against their subjects, no less than against external enemies. To prevent the weaker members of the community from being preyed upon by innumerable vultures, it was needful that there should be an animal of prey stronger than the rest, commissioned to keep them down. But as the king of the vultures would be no less bent upon preying on the flock than any of the minor harpies, it was indispensable to be in a perpetual attitude of defense against his beak and claws. The aim, therefore, of patriots was to set limits to the power which the ruler should be suffered to exercise over the community; and this limitation was what they meant by liberty. It was attempted in two ways. First, by obtaining a recognition of certain immunities, called political liberties or rights, which it was to be regarded as a breach of duty in the ruler to infringe, and which if he did infringe, specific resistance, or general rebellion, was held to be justifiable. A second, and generally a later expedient, was the establishment of constitutional checks, by which the consent of the community, or of a body of some sort, supposed to represent its interests, was made a necessary condition to some of the more important acts of the governing power. To the first of these modes of limitation, the ruling power, in most European countries, was compelled, more or less, to submit. It was not so with the second; and, to attain this, or when already in some degree possessed, to attain it more completely, became everywhere the principal object of the lovers of liberty. And so long as mankind were content to combat one enemy by another, and to be ruled by a master, on condition of being guaranteed more or less efficaciously against his tyranny, they did not carry their aspirations beyond this point.

A time, however, came, in the progress of human affairs, when men ceased to think it a necessity of nature that their governors should be an independent power, opposed in interest to themselves. It appeared to them much better that the various magistrates of the State should be their tenants or delegates, revocable at their pleasure. In that way alone, it seemed, could they have complete security that the powers of government would never be abused to their disadvantage. By degrees this new demand for elective and temporary rulers became the prominent object of the exertions of the popular party, wherever any such party existed; and superseded, to a considerable extent, the previous efforts to limit the power of rulers. As the struggle proceeded for making the ruling power emanate from the periodical choice of the ruled, some persons began to think that too much importance had been attached to the limitation of the power itself. *That* (it might seem) was a resource against rulers whose interests were habitually opposed to those of the people. What was now wanted was, that the rulers should be identified with the people; that their interest and will should be the interest and will of the nation. The nation did not need to be protected against its own will. There was no fear of its tyrannizing over itself. Let the rulers be effectually responsible to it, promptly removable by it, and it could afford to trust them with power of which it could itself dictate the use to be made. Their power was but the nation's own power, concentrated, and in a form convenient for exercise. . . .

But in political and philosophical theories, as well as in persons, success discloses faults and infirmities which failure might have concealed from observation. The notion that the people have no need to limit their power over themselves, might seem axiomatic when popular government was a thing only dreamed about, or read of as having existed at some distant period of the past. . . . In time, however, a democratic republic* came to occupy a large portion of the earth's surface, and made itself felt as one of the most powerful members of the community of nations; and elective and responsible government became subject to the observations and criticisms which wait upon a great existing fact. It was now perceived that such phrases as "self-government," and "the power of the people over themselves," do not express the true state of the case. The "people" who exercise the power are not always the same people with those over whom it is exercised; and the "self-government" spoken of is not the government of each by himself, but of each by all the rest. The will of the people, moreover, practically means the will of the most numerous or the most active *part* of the people; the majority, or those who succeed in making themselves accepted as the majority: the people, consequently *may* desire to oppress a part of their number, and precautions are as much needed against this as against any other abuse of power. The limitation, therefore, of the power of government over individuals loses none of its importance when the holders of power are regularly accountable to the community, that is, to the strongest party therein. . . . And in political speculations "the tyranny of the majority" is now generally included among the evils against which society requires to be on its guard.

---

* Mill is referring to the United States of America.

Like other tyrannies, the tyranny of the majority was at first, and is still vulgarly, held in dread chiefly as operating through the acts of the public authorities. But reflecting persons perceived that when society is itself the tyrant—society collectively over the separate individuals who compose it—its means of tyrannizing are not restricted to the acts which it may do by the hands of its political functionaries. Society can and does execute its own mandates; and if it issues wrong mandates instead of right, or any mandates at all in things with which it ought not to meddle, it practices a social tyranny more formidable than many kinds of political oppression, since, though not usually upheld by such extreme penalties, it leaves fewer means of escape, penetrating much more deeply into the details of life, and enslaving the soul itself. Protection, therefore, against the tyranny of the magistrate is not enough: there needs protection also against the tyranny of the prevailing opinion and feeling; against the tendency of society to impose, by other means than civil penalties, its own ideas and practices as rules of conduct on those who dissent from them; to fetter the development, and, if possible, prevent the formation, of any individuality not in harmony with its ways, and compels all characters to fashion themselves upon the model of its own. There is a limit to the legitimate interference of collective opinion with individual independence; and to find that limit, and maintain it against encroachment, is as indispensable to a good condition of human affairs, as protection against political despotism.

But though this proposition is not likely to be contested in general terms, the practical question, where to place the limit—how to make the fitting adjustment between individual independence and social control—is a subject on which nearly everything remains to be done. All that makes existence valuable to anyone, depends on the enforcement of restraints upon the actions of other people. Some rules of conduct, therefore, must be imposed, by law in the first place, and by opinion on many things which are not fit subjects for the operation of law. What these rules should be is the principal question in human affairs; but if we except a few of the most obvious cases, it is one of those which least progress has been made in resolving. No two ages, and scarcely any two countries, have decided it alike; and the decision of one age or country is a wonder to another. Yet the people of any given age and country no more suspect any difficulty in it, than if it were a subject on which mankind had always been agreed. The rules which obtain among themselves appear to them self-evident and self-justifying. This all but universal illusion is one of the examples of the magical influence of custom, which is not only, as the proverb says, a second nature, but is continually mistaken for the first. The effect of custom, in preventing any misgiving respecting the rules of conduct which mankind impose on one another, is all the more complete because the subject is one on which it is not generally considered necessary that reasons should be given, either by one person to others or by each to himself. People are accustomed to believe, and have been encouraged in the belief by some who aspire to the character of philosophers, that their feelings, on subjects of this nature, are better than reasons, and render reasons unnecessary. The practical principle which guides them to their opinions on the regulation of human conduct, is the feeling in each person's mind that everybody should be required to act as he, and those with whom he sympathizes, would like them to act. No one, indeed, acknowledges to himself that his standard of judgment is his own liking; but an opinion on a point of conduct, not supported by reasons, can only count as one person's preference; and if the reasons, when given, are a mere appeal to a similar preference felt by other people, it is still only many people's liking instead of one. To an ordinary man, however, his own preference, thus supported, is not only a perfectly satisfactory reason, but the only one he generally has for any of his notions of morality, taste, or propriety, which are not expressly written in his religious creed; and his chief guide in the interpretation even of that. Men's opinions, accordingly, on what is laudable or blamable, are affected by all the multifarious causes which influence their wishes in regard to the conduct of others, and which are as numerous as those which determine their wishes on any subject. Sometimes their reason, at other times their prejudices or superstitions; often their social affections, not seldom their antisocial ones, their envy or jealousy, their arrogance or contemptuousness: but most commonly their desires or fears for themselves—their legitimate or illegitimate self-interest. Wherever there is an ascendant class, a large portion of the morality of the country emanates from its class interests, and its feelings of class superiority. . . .

The likings and dislikings of society, or of some powerful portion of it, are thus the main thing which has practically determined the rules laid down for general observance, under the penalties of law or opinion. And in general, those who have been in advance of society in thought and feeling, have left this condition of things unassailed in principle, however they may have come into conflict with it in some of its details. They have occupied themselves rather in inquiring what things society ought to like or dislike, than in questioning whether its likings or dislikings should be a law to individuals. They preferred endeavoring to alter the feelings of mankind on the particular points on which they were themselves heretical, rather than make common cause in defense of freedom, with heretics generally. . . .

The object of this essay is to assert one very simple principle, as entitled to govern absolutely the dealings of society with the individual in the way of compulsion and control, whether the means used be physical force in the form of legal penalties, or the moral coercion of public opinion. That principle is, that the sole end for which mankind are warranted, individually or collectively, in interfering with the liberty of action of any of their number, is self-protection. That the only purpose for which power can be rightfully exercised over any member of a civilized community, against his will, is to prevent harm to others. His own good, either physical or moral, is not a sufficient warrant. He cannot rightfully be compelled to do or forbear because it will be better for him to do so, because it will make him happier, because, in the opinions of others, to do so would be wise, or even right. These are good reasons for remonstrating with him, or reasoning with him, or persuading him, or entreating him, but not for compelling him, or visiting him with any evil in case he do otherwise. To justify that, the conduct from which it is desired to deter him must be calculated to produce evil to someone else. The only part of the conduct of anyone, for which he is amenable to society, is that which concerns others. In the part which merely concerns himself, his independence is, of right, absolute. Over himself, over his own body and mind, the individual is sovereign.

It is perhaps hardly necessary to say that this doctrine is meant to apply only to human beings in the maturity of their faculties. We are not speaking of children, or of young persons below the age which the law may fix as that of manhood or womanhood. Those who are still in a state to require being taken care of by others, must be protected against their own actions as well as against external injury. . . . But as soon as [mankind] have attained the capacity of being guided to their own improvement by conviction or persuasion . . . , compulsion, either in the direct form or in that of pains and penalties for non-compliance, is no longer admissible as a means to their own good, and justifiable only for the security of others.

It is proper to state that I forego any advantage which could be derived to my argument from the idea of abstract right, as a thing independent of utility. I regard utility as the ultimate appeal on all ethical questions; but it must be utility in the largest sense, grounded on the permanent interests of a man as a progressive being. Those interests, I contend, authorized the subjection of individual spontaneity to external control, only in respect to those actions of each which concern the interest of other people. If anyone does an act hurtful to others, there is a *prima facie* case for punishing him, by law, or, where legal penalties are not safely applicable, by general disapprobation. There are also many positive acts for the benefit of others, which he may rightfully be compelled to perform: such as to give evidence in a court of justice; to bear his fair share in the common defense, or in any other joint work necessary to the interest of the society of which he enjoys the protection; and to perform certain acts of individual beneficence, such as saving a fellow creature's life, or interposing to protect the defenseless against ill usage, things which whenever it is obviously a man's duty to do, he may rightfully be made responsible to society for not doing. A person may cause evil to others not only by his actions but by his inaction, and in either case he is justly accountable to them for the injury. . . .

But there is a sphere of action in which society, as distinguished from the individual, has, if any, only an indirect interest; comprehending all that portion of a person's life and conduct which affects only himself, or if it also affects others, only with their free, voluntary, and undeceived consent and participation. When I say only himself, I mean directly, and in the first instance; for whatever affects himself, may affect others through himself; and the objection which may be grounded on this contingency, will receive consideration in the sequel. This, then, is the appropriate region of human liberty. It comprises, *first,* the inward domain of consciousness; demanding liberty of conscience in the most comprehensive sense; liberty of thought and feeling; absolute freedom of opinion and sentiment on all subjects, practical or speculative, scientific, moral, or theological. The liberty of expressing and publishing opinions may seem to fall under a different principle, since it belongs to that part of the conduct of an individual which concerns other people; but, being almost of as much importance as the liberty of thought itself, and resting in great part on the same reasons, is practically inseparable from it. *Secondly,* the principle requires liberty of tastes and pursuits; of framing the plan of our life to suit our own character; of doing as we like, subject to such consequences as may follow: without impediment from our fellow creatures, so long as what we do does not harm them, even though they should think our conduct foolish, perverse, or wrong. *Thirdly,* from this liberty of each individual, follows the liberty, within the same limits, of combination among individuals; freedom to unite, for any purpose not involving harm to others: the persons combining being supposed to be of full age, and not forced or deceived.

No society in which these liberties are not, on the whole, respected, is free, whatever may be its form of government; and none is completely free in which they do not exist absolute and unqualified. The only freedom which deserves the name, is that of pursuing our own good in our own way, so long as we do not attempt to deprive others of theirs, or impede their efforts to obtain it. Each is the proper guardian of his own health, whether bodily, or mental and spiritual. Mankind are greater gainers by suffering each other to live as seems good to themselves, than by compelling each to live as seems good to the rest.

Though this doctrine is anything but new, and, to some persons, may have the air of a truism, there is no doctrine which stands more directly opposed to the general tendency of existing opinion and practice. Society has expended fully as much effort in the attempt (according to its lights) to compel people to conform to its notions of personal as of social excellence. . . .

. . . There is also in the world at large an increasing inclination to stretch unduly the powers of society over the individual, both by the force of opinion and even by that of legislation; and as the tendency of all the changes taking place in the world is to strengthen society, and diminish the power of the individual, this encroachment is not one of the evils which tend spontaneously to disappear, but, on the contrary, to grow more and more formidable. The disposition of mankind, whether as rulers or as fellow citizens, to impose their own opinions and inclinations as a rule of conduct on others, is so energetically supported by some of the best and by some of the worst feelings incident to human nature, that it is hardly ever kept under restraint by anything but want of power; and as the power is not declining, but growing, unless a strong barrier of moral conviction can be raised against the mischief, we must expect, in the present circumstances of the world, to see it increase. . . .

■■

Interpretive Questions

1. Is it an advantage to the society if individuals are allowed to live as seems good to themselves?

2. How can moral conviction block the pressure society exerts to make all people conform to its rules of conduct?

3. Why does Mill make the test for maturity the capacity of being improved through conviction or persuasion?

4. Why does Mill call the influence of custom "magical"?

5. Why does Mill think that society's likes and dislikes should not be a law of behavior for individuals?

VI

By and About Immanuel Kant

(1724–1804)

Immanuel Kant characterized true philosophy as "the ability to think and to inquire into the nature of things on one's own without any preconceived biases and without any dependence on sectarian doctrine." Enlightenment, he said, is

man's emergence from his self-imposed nonage. Nonage is the inability to use one's own understanding without another's guidance. This nonage is self-imposed if its cause lies not in lack of understanding but in indecision and lack of courage to use one's own mind without another's guidance. *Dare to know!*

Kant spent his entire life within sixty miles of the University of Königsberg, where he wrote:

I am by nature an explorer. I feel an unquenchable thirst for knowledge and a restless desire to acquire it, as well as the satisfaction that comes with every step forward in an investigation. There was a time when I believed that all this could bring honor to mankind and I despised the vulgar who know nothing. . . . [But] the illusion of superior merit disappeared; I learned to respect all human beings and would consider myself less useful than a common laborer did I not believe that this observation might bring value to everything else by reestablishing the rights of mankind.

According to Kant:

Man and generally any rational being exists as an end in himself, not merely as a means to be arbitrarily used by this or that will, but in all his actions, whether they concern himself or other rational beings, must be always regarded at the same time as an end.

He held that the supreme principle of ethics is:

> Act on the maxim, the *ends* of which are such as it might be a universal law for everyone to have. On this principle a man is an end to himself as well as others, and it is not enough that he is not permitted to use either himself or others merely as means (which would imply that he might be indifferent to them), but it is in itself a duty of every man to make mankind in general his end.

In his lecture on conscience, Kant distinguishes between an instinct of judgment and a faculty of judgment. A faculty of judgment is a power of judgment we are free to exercise or not, depending on our feelings: we can decide to blame ourselves for some action or not pass judgment at all. An instinct of judgment, on the other hand, is a judgment we must make whether we want to or not. Conscience is an instinct of judgment because it has the power to summon us against our will. According to Kant, such judgments are made on the basis of moral law—a basic sense of right and wrong possessed by anyone who can reason.

Kant views judgments made by conscience as judicial rather than logical. A logical judgment is merely formed: we may form a judgment about some book we have read or some action we have performed. A judicial judgment is a judgment that can be enforced: conscience can either acquit us or declare us guilty and impose a sentence.

Conscience

Immanuel Kant

Conscience is an instinct to pass judgment upon ourselves
in accordance with moral laws. It is not a mere faculty, but an
instinct; and its judgment is not logical, but judicial. We have
the faculty to judge ourselves logically in terms of laws of
morality; we can make such use as we please of this faculty.
But conscience has the power to summon us against our will
before the judgment seat to be judged on account of the righ-
teousness or unrighteousness of our actions. It is thus an instinct and not merely a faculty of judgment, and it is an instinct
to judge, not in the logical, but in the judicial sense.

A judge passes judgment; he does not merely form a judgment. The difference is that he has the right to judge with
authority, and to give legal effect to his judgment. Thus his
judgment has force of law, and is a sentence. The judge must
either condemn or acquit, not merely form a judgment.

If our conscience were merely an impulse to form a judgment, it would be, like other faculties of which we are

possessed (e.g. the impulses to compare ourselves with others, or to flatter ourselves), a faculty of knowledge. We all have an impulse to pat ourselves on the back for good actions done in accordance with rules of prudence. We likewise reproach ourselves for imprudent conduct. Thus we all have an impulse to flatter and blame ourselves in accordance with rules of prudence. But this tendency to praise and blame oneself is not conscience, though it is analogous to it and men often mistake it for conscience.

A criminal lying under sentence of death frets and worries and reproaches himself severely, but mainly for the imprudence which led to detection. He imagines that it is his conscience which reproaches him for his immorality; but it is not the pangs of conscience that he feels; for, had he got off scot-free, he would feel its reproach in any event. We must, therefore, differentiate between the judgment of prudence and the judgment of conscience.

Many people have only a semblance of conscience which they imagine is conscience itself. Deathbed repentance is a case in point. Such repentance is often enough not remorse for the immorality of behavior, but for the folly of actions which, now that the judgment seat is near, make it impossible to stand before the judge.

Vices bring their own punishments, and these punishments bring home to us the criminality of the acts; a man, therefore, who feels disgust with his past vices does not know whether his loathing is due to the punishments or to the criminality of his offenses.

He who has no immediate loathing for what is morally wicked, and finds no pleasure in what is morally good, has no moral feeling, and such a man has no conscience. He who goes in fear of being prosecuted for a wicked deed, does not reproach himself on the score of the wickedness of his misdemeanor, but on the score of the painful consequences which await him; such a one has no conscience, but only a semblance of it. But he who has a sense of the wickedness of the deed itself, be the consequences what they may, has a conscience.

We must guard against confusion here: reproaches for the consequences of imprudence must not be confused with reproaches for breaches of morality. . . .

Prudence reproaches; conscience accuses. If a man has acted unwisely and reproaches himself for his imprudence no longer than is necessary for him to learn his lesson, he is observing a rule of prudence and it must be accounted to him for honor, for it is a sign of strength of character. But the accusation of conscience cannot be so readily dismissed, neither should it be; it is not a matter of the will, and the capacity to dismiss the accusation of a remorseful conscience is no evidence of strength of character, but rather of wickedness and religious impenitence. A man who can at will dismiss the accusations of conscience is a rebel, like the man who can disregard the accusation of his judge, over whom the judge has no power. . . .

The judgment has validity if it is felt and enforced. Two consequences follow from this. The first effectual expression of this judicial verdict which has the force of law is moral repentance; the second, without which the sentence is inoperative, is action in accordance with the judicial verdict. If it does not result in practical endeavor to do what is demanded for the satisfaction of the moral law, the conscience is but an idle conscience, and however penitent we may be the penitence is vain so long as we do not satisfy the debt we owe to the moral law; for even in the human sphere a debt is not satisfied by penitence, but by payment. . . . The history of deathbed repentances can, of course, show no instance of such practical repentance—a proof that it neglects an essential element.

The court of justice of our conscience can conveniently be

compared with an ordinary lawcourt. We find in our hearts a prosecutor, for whom there would be no place unless there were also a law. This law, which is based on reason and not on sentiment, is incorruptible and incontestably just and pure; it is the moral law, established as the holy and inviolable law of humanity. Beside these there is equally an advocate within us, called Self-love, who brings forward many an argument in our defense, and whose pleas the prosecutor in his turn endeavors to refute. Lastly we find a judge within us who either condemns or acquits. It is impossible to blind his judgment. To refuse to appear before the bar of conscience is easier. Once we appear, the judge pronounces impartially, and his verdict falls normally upon the side of truth. If not, it must be because he judges by false principles of morality.

Except on the deathbed, when they listen more eagerly to the accuser, men lend a readier ear to their defender. A good conscience demands a pure law, for the accuser must be on the watch, whatever we do; and in judging our actions we must judge justly and morally and must have strength of conscience to give effect to the valid judgment. The conscience must have its operative, and not merely its speculative, principles; and to make its judgments operative it must be strong and command respect. Where is the judge who would be content to do no more than lecture and make judicial pronouncements? Judicial pronouncements must be put into operation.

Let us consider wherein the just conscience differs from one that is at fault. An error of conscience can be either an error of fact or an error of law. If a man's conscience errs and he acts in accordance with it, his acts may be at fault, but they cannot be accounted to him for a transgression. There are blameworthy errors and innocent errors. In respect of his natural obligations no man can be at fault; the natural moral laws must be known to all; they are contained in our reason; no man can, therefore, err innocently in respect of them, and in the case of natural laws there can be no innocent errors; but it is otherwise with positive laws; here we can have innocent errors; and an erring conscience may give rise to actions which are not culpable. In respect of the natural law there can be no innocent errors.

But what is a man to do when a positive and a natural law conflict? Take, for instance, the case of a man who is taught by his religion to execrate adherents of other religions, or that of a man who is told by Jesuits that good can come from knavery. Such a man would not be acting in accord with his conscience; the natural law is known to him, and he is aware that he ought on no account to act unrighteously. The verdict of natural conscience being in conflict with the verdict of instructed conscience, he must obey the former.

All positive laws are conditioned by the natural law, and they cannot, therefore, rightly contain anything which conflicts with it. To plead the excuse of an erring conscience is a serious matter, for in this way we could shift the responsibility for a great deal; but we are also accountable for our errors. . . .

Conscience is the representative within us of the divine judgment seat: it weighs our dispositions and actions in the scales of a law which is holy and pure; we cannot deceive it, and, lastly, we cannot escape it because, like the divine omnipresence, it is always with us. Since, then, conscience is the representative within us of divine justice, we must not hurt or injure it.

We might contrast natural conscience and artificial conscience. Many have argued that conscience is a work of art and education, and that it judges and sentences by force of habit; but if this were the case, men with a conscience not so tutored and practiced could escape the stings of conscience; there are, however, no cases of this.

It is obvious that art and instruction can only bring into fruition that for which we have a natural aptitude, so that if our conscience is to judge we must have a prior knowledge of good and evil. Yet a cultivated mind need not be followed by a cultivated conscience. Thus conscience is synonymous with natural conscience; and if we are to draw distinctions it should be between conscience before, during, and after the act.

Before the act the conscience has power enough to dissuade a man from committing the act, during the act it is stronger, and it is strongest of all after the act. Before the act conscience must still be weak; for the act has not yet been committed, and we feel weaker in the presence of an unsatisfied inclination which is still strong enough to withstand conscience. During the act conscience becomes stronger; and then, when inclination is satisfied, and has become too weak to withstand conscience, conscience is at its strongest. We can see from the case of passion that after satisfying his strongest desire, a man is even overcome by a feeling of disgust, because a strong passion, once satisfied, becomes too languid to offer opposition, so that conscience is at its strongest, and remorse follows. . . .

Conscience accompanying the act is gradually weakened by usage, so that in the long run man becomes as used to his vices as to tobacco smoke. In the end his conscience loses all its authority, the court of justice ceases to function and decide, and the accuser has no longer any task to perform.

Some burden their conscience with many matters of negligible importance; they ask it to resolve problems of a quibbling nature, such as whether it is right to tell a lie in order to make an April fool of a person, or whether a rite or ceremony should be performed in this or that manner. This is casuistry, and it produces a micrological conscience. The subtler conscience is in such matters of detail, the worse is it in matters of practical importance, and people with such consciences are notoriously wont to concern themselves with speculations arising from positive law and to give themselves a free hand in everything else.

If a person is capable of reproaching himself for his sins, his conscience is said to be alive; but on the other hand, if a man searches needlessly for evidences of evil in his conduct, his conscience is melancholy. Conscience should not lord it over us like a tyrant; we do no hurt to our conscience by proceeding on our way cheerfully; tormenting consciences in the long run become dulled and ultimately cease to function.

Interpretive Questions

1. How does a person know the natural law, as Kant says he does, if the law isn't written down?

2. In Kant's image of conscience as court of justice, is conscience the prosecutor, the advocate, and the judge, or just the judge?

3. Why do some people have a developed conscience whereas others do not?

4. Can a person be sure that conscience, rather than prudence, is controlling his or her feelings of remorse?

5. If conscience is an instinct, how can we refuse to appear before the bar of conscience?

ERPRETA
EVALUATIO
TION FA
FACT IN
ON EVALU
JATION FA
RETATIO
FACT INT
VALUATION
NTERPRE
CT EVALUA
RETATIO
ATION FA
ERPRETA
FACT EVA
ON FACT
ATION INT
FACT EVA
ERPRETA
ALUATION
RETATIO
FACT IN
NTERPRE
ATION INT
TATION

Questions of Fact, Interpretation, and Evaluation

Three kinds of questions are asked about a selection in shared inquiry: questions of fact, questions of interpretation, and questions of evaluation.

Questions of fact ask you to recall something in the selection, using your own words or the words of the author. A question of fact has only one correct answer.

Questions of interpretation ask you to offer your opinion about what the selection means. Unlike a question of fact, a question of interpretation usually has more than one correct answer.

Questions of evaluation ask you whether you agree or disagree with what the author said or whether something in the selection has application to your own life. You support your answer to a question of evaluation by talking about your own values or your own experiences rather than about the selection itself.

Since interpreting literature is the main purpose of the Great Books program, discussion focuses on questions of interpretation. Factual questions are used to bring out evidence in support of interpretations. Questions of evaluation are asked only after the meaning of a selection has been clarified through discussion.

This exercise will give you practice in distinguishing questions of fact, interpretation, and evaluation. In the blank before each of the following questions, write (F) if the question is FACTUAL, (I) if it is INTERPRETIVE, or (E) if it is EVALUATIVE. If you are in doubt about how to classify any question, refer to the selection.

_____ 1. Why does a tormenting conscience eventually cease to function?

_____ 2. Why is conscience like a judge?

_____ 3. What keeps you honest, your conscience or your fear of being punished?

_____ 4. Is it your conscience that tells you when other people are doing something wrong?

_____ 5. Why can conscience condemn or acquit, but not reward?

_____ 6. What is the difference between prudence and conscience?

_____ 7. Why is it difficult to maintain a strong conscience, according to Kant?

_____ 8. Why is the voice of conscience often stronger in telling us what we should *not* do than in telling us what we should do?

_____ 9. Why does a deathbed repentence usually have no moral worth, according to Kant?

_____ 10. Why does conscience require an immediate loathing for what is wicked?

VII

Getting Into a Story

In our daily lives we often have to act before we understand; there is seldom time for simply feeling or seeing. But a story provides an opportunity for such reflection and a release from our usual responsibilities. It invites us to step outside ourselves—to set aside our prejudices and opinions and see what the world looks like from another angle of vision.

As we read a story, we observe the characters in their most private moments. We eavesdrop on their conversations and learn their innermost thoughts. Yet they pay us no mind, and no matter how intense our involvement, we never quite forget that they exist in a realm beyond our help. Since we stand neither to gain nor to lose by what goes on in a story, we can suspend judgment in favor of understanding. Reading a story is a way to participate, without risk, in another world.

Before we can enter the world of a story, we must first bring it to life in our minds. Envisioning a story—recreating an author's world in our own imagination—begins with an alertness to details and a sensuous or artistic appreciation of them. The details of a story guide reflection, anchoring our thoughts and feelings. They also serve, with our assistance, to bring characters and scenes to life.

Since writers seldom spell everything out for their readers, getting into a story involves not only collecting details, but a process of inference as well. For example, it would be a pointless exercise for even a very talented writer to attempt to describe a character completely. What he does instead is give us the most revealing or meaningful details. In fiction, the salient features of a face are apt to correspond to a character's inner world or to suggest something of his meaning for an author. With repetition and emphasis, physical facts may take on symbolic value.

In the best stories, each detail is carefully chosen not only for its power to evoke reality, but also as a guide to meaningful reflection. Our first priority, then, is to gather the "sunny trifles" of the story—to savor its concrete details. Through them the world of the story comes into being: the atmosphere builds and the shadowy figures of the author's imagination take on flesh. If these characters and their world possess what a poet called a "semblance of truth and sufficient human interest," they win our credence, or a "willing suspension of disbelief for the moment." Then we cease to be aware of the effort we are expending as we read. Our curiosity carries us through the story, which we read with passion and understanding. ■▮

By and About Franz Kafka

(1883–1924)

After earning a doctorate in law—the profession offering him "the widest scope for indifference"—Franz Kafka began a successful career at an insurance institute. By night he wrote novels and stories. Kafka was released from the strain of this "double life" when tuberculosis forced him to retire in 1922. He died two years later, hoping that none of his work would remain in print.

A passionate reader who enjoyed reading aloud from his favorite authors, Kafka looked to books for much more than pleasure or even happiness. He confided to a friend:

> I believe that we should read only those books that bite and sting us. If a book we are reading does not rouse us with a blow to the head, then why read it? Because it will make us happy, you tell me? My God, we would also be happy if we had no books, and the kind of books that make us happy we could, if necessary, write ourselves. What we need are books that affect us like some really grievous misfortune, like the death of one whom we loved more than ourselves, as if we were banished to distant forests, away from everybody, like a suicide; a book must be the ax for the frozen sea within us.

Through words, Kafka believed, we discover ourselves. Moreover, he refused to admit that perfect self-expression might ever be impossible:

> Observations on the weakness of language, and comparisons between the limitations of words and the infinity of feelings, are quite fallacious. The infinite feeling continues to be as infinite in words as it was in the heart. What is clear within is bound to become so in words as well. This is why one need never worry about oneself. After all, who knows within himself how things really are with him? This tempestuous or floundering of morass-like inner self is what we really are, but by the secret process by which words are forced out of us, our self-knowledge is brought

to light, and though it may still be veiled, yet it is there before us, wonderful or terrible to behold.

Kafka valued art because it allows human beings "to speak truth to one another." Writing, he said

means revealing oneself to excess; that utmost of self-revelation and surrender, in which a human being, when involved with others, would feel he was losing himself, and from which, therefore, he will always shrink as long as he is in his right mind . . . even that degree of self-revelation and surrender is not enough for writing. Writing that springs from the surface of existence—when there is no other way and the deeper wells have dried up—is nothing, and collapses the moment a truer emotion makes that surface shake. This is why one can never be alone enough when one writes, why there can never be enough silence around one when one writes, why even night is not night enough.

A Hunger Artist

Franz Kafka

During these last decades the interest in professional fasting has markedly diminished. It used to pay very well to stage such great performances under one's own management, but today that is quite impossible. We live in a different world now. At one time the whole town took a lively interest in the hunger artist; from day to day of his fast the excitement mounted; everybody wanted to see him at least once a day; there were people who bought season tickets for the last few days and sat from morning till night in front of his small barred cage; even in the nighttime there were visiting hours, when the whole effect was heightened by torch flares; on fine days the cage was set out in the open air, and then it was the children's special treat to see the hunger artist; for their elders he was often just a joke that happened to be in fashion, but the children stood openmouthed, holding each other's hands for greater security, marveling at him as he sat there pallid in black tights, with his ribs sticking out so prominently, not even on a seat but down among straw on the ground, sometimes giving a courteous nod, answering questions with a constrained smile, or perhaps stretching an arm through the bars so that one might feel how thin it was, and then again withdrawing deep into himself, paying no attention to anyone or anything, not even to the all-important striking of the clock that was the only piece of furniture in his cage, but merely staring into vacancy with half-shut eyes, now and then taking a sip from a tiny glass of water to moisten his lips.

Besides casual onlookers there were also relays of permanent watchers selected by the public, usually butchers, strangely enough, and it was their task to watch the hunger artist day and night, three of them at a time, in case he should have some secret recourse to nourishment. This was nothing but a formality, instituted to reassure the masses, for the initiates knew well enough that during his fast the artist would never in any circumstances, not even under forcible compulsion, swallow the smallest morsel of food; the honor of his profession forbade it. Not every watcher, of course, was capable of understanding this, there were often groups of night watchers who were very lax in carrying out their duties and deliberately huddled together in a retired corner to play cards with great absorption, obviously intending to give the hunger artist the chance of a little refreshment, which they supposed he could draw from some private hoard. Nothing annoyed the artist more than such watchers; they made him miserable; they made his fast seem unendurable; sometimes he mastered his feebleness sufficiently to sing during their watch for as long as he could keep going, to show them how unjust their suspicions were. But that was of little use; they only wondered at his cleverness in being able to fill his mouth even while singing. Much more to his taste were the watchers who sat close up to the bars, who were not content with the dim night lighting of the hall but focused him in the full glare of the electric pocket torch given them by the impresario. The harsh light did not trouble him at all, in any case he could never sleep properly, and he could always drowse a little, whatever the light, at any hour, even when the hall was thronged with noisy onlookers. He was quite happy at the prospect of spending a sleepless night with such watchers; he was ready to exchange jokes with them, to tell them stories out of his nomadic life, anything at all to keep them awake and demonstrate to them again that he had no eatables in his cage and that he was fasting as not one of them could fast. But his happiest moment was when the morning came and an enormous breakfast was brought them, at his expense, on which they flung themselves with the keen appetite of healthy men after a weary night of wakefulness. Of course there were people who argued that this breakfast was an unfair attempt to bribe the watchers, but that was going rather too far, and when they were invited to take on a night's vigil without a breakfast, merely for the sake of the cause, they made themselves scarce, although they stuck stubbornly to their suspicions.

Such suspicions, anyhow, were a necessary accompaniment to the profession of fasting. No one could possibly watch the hunger artist continuously, day and night, and so no one could produce first-hand evidence that the fast had really been rigorous and continuous; only the artist himself could know that, he was therefore bound to be the sole completely satisfied spectator of his own fast. Yet for other reasons he was never satisfied; it was not perhaps mere fasting that had brought him to such skeleton thinness that many people had regretfully to keep away from his exhibitions, because the sight of him was too much for them, perhaps it was dissatisfaction with himself that had worn him down. For he alone knew, what no other

initiate knew, how easy it was to fast. It was the easiest thing
in the world. He made no secret of this, yet people did not
believe him, at the best they set him down as modest; most of
them, however, thought he was out for publicity or else was
some kind of cheat who found it easy to fast because he had
discovered a way of making it easy, and then had the impudence to admit the fact, more or less. He had to put up with
all that, and in the course of time had got used to it, but his
inner dissatisfaction always rankled, and never yet, after any
term of fasting—this must be granted to his credit—had he left
the cage of his own free will. The longest period of fasting was
fixed by his impresario at forty days, beyond that term he was
not allowed to go, not even in great cities, and there was good
reason for it, too. Experience had proved that for about forty
days the interest of the public could be stimulated by a steadily
increasing pressure of advertisement, but after that the town
began to lose interest, sympathetic support began notably to
fall off; there were of course local variations as between one
town and another or one country and another, but as a general
rule forty days marked the limit. So on the fortieth day the
flower-bedecked cage was opened, enthusiastic spectators filled
the hall, a military band played, two doctors entered the cage
to measure the results of the fast, which were announced
through a megaphone, and finally two young ladies appeared,
blissful at having been selected for the honor, to help the
hunger artist down the few steps leading to a small table on
which was spread a carefully chosen invalid repast. And at this
very moment the artist always turned stubborn. True, he would
entrust his bony arms to the outstretched helping hands of the
ladies bending over him, but stand up he would not. Why stop
fasting at this particular moment, after forty days of it? He had
held out for a long time, an illimitably long time; why stop
now, when he was in his best fasting form, or rather, not yet

quite in his best fasting form? Why should he be cheated of the fame he would get for fasting longer, for being not only the record hunger artist of all time, which presumably he was already, but for beating his own record by a performance beyond human imagination, since he felt that there were no limits to his capacity for fasting? His public pretended to admire him so much, why should it have so little patience with him; if he could endure fasting longer, why shouldn't the public endure it? Besides, he was tired, he was comfortable sitting in the straw, and now he was supposed to lift himself to his full height and go down to a meal the very thought of which gave him a nausea that only the presence of the ladies kept him from betraying, and even that with an effort. And he looked up into the eyes of the ladies who were apparently so friendly and in reality so cruel, and shook his head, which felt too heavy on its strengthless neck. But then there happened yet again what always happened. The impresario came forward, without a word—for the band made speech impossible—lifted his arms in the air above the artist, as if inviting Heaven to look down upon its creature here in the straw, this suffering martyr, which indeed he was, although in quite another sense; grasped him around the emaciated waist, with exaggerated caution, so that the frail condition he was in might be appreciated; and committed him to the care of the blenching ladies, not without secretly giving him a shaking so that his legs and body tottered and swayed. The artist now submitted completely; his head lolled on his breast as if it had landed there by chance; his body was hollowed out; his legs in a spasm of self-preservation clung close to each other at the knees, yet scraped on the ground as if it were not really solid ground, as if they were only trying to find solid ground; and the whole weight of his body, a featherweight after all, relapsed onto one of the ladies, who, looking around for help and panting a little—this post of honor was not at all what she had expected it to be—first stretched her neck as far as she could to keep her face at least free from contact with the artist, then finding this impossible, and her more fortunate companion not coming to her aid but merely holding extended in her own trembling hand the little bunch of knucklebones that was the artist's, to the great delight of the spectators burst into tears and had to be replaced by an attendant who had long been stationed in readiness. Then came the food, a little of which the impresario managed to get between the artist's lips, while he sat in a kind of half-fainting trance, to the accompaniment of cheerful patter designed to distract the public's attention from the artist's condition; after that, a toast was drunk to the public, supposedly prompted by a whisper from the artist in the impresario's ear; the band confirmed it with a mighty flourish, the spectators melted away, and no one had any cause to be dissatisfied with the proceedings, no one except the hunger artist himself, he only, as always.

So he lived for many years, with small regular intervals of recuperation, in visible glory, honored by the world, yet in spite of that troubled in spirit, and all the more troubled because no one would take his trouble seriously. What comfort could he possibly need? What more could he possibly wish for? And if some good-natured person, feeling sorry for him, tried to console him by pointing out that his melancholy was probably caused by fasting, it could happen, especially when he had been fasting for some time, that he reacted with an outburst of fury and to the general alarm began to shake the bars of his cage like a wild animal. Yet the impresario had a way of punishing these outbreaks which he rather enjoyed putting into operation. He would apologize publicly for the artist's behavior, which was only to be excused, he admitted, because of the irritability caused by fasting; a condition hardly to be understood by well-fed people; then by natural transition he went on to mention the artist's equally incomprehensible boast that he could fast for much longer than he was doing; he praised the high ambition, the goodwill, the great self-denial undoubtedly implicit in such a statement; and then quite simply countered it by bringing out photographs, which were also on sale to the public, showing the artist on the fortieth day of a fast lying in bed almost dead from exhaustion. This perversion of the truth, familiar to the artist though it was, always unnerved him afresh and proved too much for him. What was a consequence of the premature ending of his fast was here presented as the cause of it! To fight against this lack of understanding, against a whole world of nonunderstanding, was impossible. Time and again in good faith he stood by the bars listening to the impresario, but as soon as the photographs appeared he always let go and sank with a groan back onto his straw, and the reassured public could once more come close and gaze at him.

A few years later when the witnesses of such scenes called them to mind, they often failed to understand themselves at all. For meanwhile the aforementioned change in public interest had set in; it seemed to happen almost overnight; there may have been profound causes for it, but who was going to bother about that; at any rate the pampered hunger artist suddenly found himself deserted one fine day by the amusement-seekers, who went streaming past him to other more-favored attractions. For the last time the impresario hurried him over half Europe to discover whether the old interest might still survive here and there; all in vain; everywhere, as if by secret agreement, a positive revulsion from professional fasting was in evidence. Of course it could not really have sprung up so suddenly as all that, and many premonitory symptoms which had not been sufficiently remarked or suppressed during the rush and glitter of success now came retrospectively to mind, but it was now too late to take any countermeasures. Fasting would surely come into fashion again at some future date, yet that was no comfort for those living in the present. What, then, was the hunger artist to do? He had been applauded by thousands in his time and could hardly come down to showing himself in a street booth at village fairs, and as for adopting another profession, he was not only too old for that but too fanatically devoted to fasting. So he took leave of the impresario, his partner in an unparalleled career, and hired himself to a large circus; in order to spare his own feelings he avoided reading the conditions of his contract.

A large circus with its enormous traffic in replacing and recruiting men, animals, and apparatus can always find a use for people at any time, even for a hunger artist, provided of course that he does not ask too much, and in this particular case anyhow it was not only the artist who was taken on but his famous and long-known name as well, indeed considering the peculiar nature of his performance, which was not impaired by advancing age, it could not be objected that here was an artist past his prime, no longer at the height of his professional skill, seeking a refuge in some quiet corner of a circus; on the contrary, the hunger artist averred that he could fast as well as ever, which was entirely credible, he even alleged that if he were allowed to fast as he liked, and this was at once promised him without more ado, he could astound the world by establishing a record never yet achieved, a statement that certainly provoked a smile among the other professionals, since it left out of account the change in public opinion, which the hunger artist in his zeal conveniently forgot.

He had not, however, actually lost his sense of the real situation and took it as a matter of course that he and his cage should be stationed, not in the middle of the ring as a main attraction, but outside, near the animal cages, on a site that was after all easily accessible. Large and gaily painted placards made a frame for the cage and announced what was to be seen inside it. When the public came thronging out in the intervals to see the animals, they could hardly avoid passing the hunger artist's cage and stopping there for a moment, perhaps they might even have stayed longer had not those pressing behind them in the narrow gangway, who did not understand why they should be held up on their way toward the excitements of the menagerie, made it impossible for anyone to stand gazing quietly for any length of time. And that was the reason why the hunger artist, who had of course been looking forward to these visiting hours as the main achievement of his life, began instead to shrink from them. At first he could hardly wait for the intervals; it was exhilarating to watch the crowds come streaming his way, until only too soon—not even the most obstinate self-deception, clung to almost consciously, could hold out against the fact—the conviction was borne in upon him that these people, most of them, to judge from their actions, again and again, without exception, were all on their way to the menagerie. And the first sight of them from the distance remained the best. For when they reached his cage he was at once deafened by the storm of shouting and abuse that arose from the two contending factions, which renewed themselves continuously, of those who wanted to stop and stare at him—he soon began to dislike them more than the others— not out of real interest but only out of obstinate self-assertiveness, and those who wanted to go straight on to the animals. When the first great rush was past, the stragglers came along, and these, whom nothing could have prevented from stopping to look at him as long as they had breath, raced past with long strides, hardly even glancing at him, in their haste to get to the menagerie in time. And all too rarely did it happen that he had a stroke of luck, when some father of a family fetched up before him with his children, pointed a finger at the hunger artist, and explained at length what the phenomenon meant, telling stories of earlier years when he himself had watched similar but much more thrilling performances, and the children, still rather uncomprehending, since neither inside nor outside school had they been sufficiently prepared for this lesson—what did they care about fasting?—yet showed by the brightness of their intent eyes that new and better times might be coming. Perhaps, said the hunger artist to himself many a time, things would be a little better if his cage were set not quite so near the menagerie. That made it too easy for people to make their choice, to say nothing of what he suffered from the stench of the menagerie, the animals' restlessness by night, the carrying past of raw lumps of flesh for the beasts of prey, the roaring at feeding times, which depressed him continually. But he did not dare to lodge a complaint with the management; after all, he had the animals to thank for the troops of people who passed his cage, among whom there might always be one here and there to take an interest in him, and who could tell where they might seclude him if he called attention to his existence and thereby to the fact that, strictly speaking, he was only an impediment on the way to the menagerie.

A small impediment, to be sure, one that grew steadily less. People grew familiar with the strange idea that they could be expected, in times like these, to take an interest in a hunger artist, and with this familiarity the verdict went out against him. He might fast as much as he could, and he did so; but nothing could save him now, people passed him by. Just try to explain to anyone the art of fasting! Anyone who has no feeling for it cannot be made to understand it. The fine placards grew dirty and illegible, they were torn down; the little notice board telling the number of fast days achieved, which at first was changed carefully every day, had long stayed at the same figure, for after the first few weeks even this small task seemed pointless to the staff; and so the artist simply fasted on and on, as he had once dreamed of doing, and it was no trouble to him, just as he had always foretold, but no one counted the days, no one, not even the artist himself, knew what records he was already breaking, and his heart grew heavy. And when once in a while some leisurely passer-by stopped, made merry over the old figure on the board, and spoke of swindling, that was in its way the stupidest lie ever invented by indifference and inborn malice, since it was not the hunger artist who was cheating, he was working honestly, but the world was cheating him of his reward.

Many more days went by, however, and that too came to an end. An overseer's eye fell on the cage one day and he asked the attendants why this perfectly good cage should be left standing there unused with dirty straw inside it; nobody knew, until one man, helped out by the notice board, remembered about the hunger artist. They poked into the straw with sticks and found him in it. "Are you still fasting?" asked the overseer, "when on earth do you mean to stop?" "Forgive me, everybody," whispered the hunger artist; only the overseer, who had his ear to the bars, understood him. "Of course," said the overseer, and tapped his forehead with a finger to let the attendants know what state the man was in, "we forgive you." "I always wanted you to admire my fasting," said the hunger artist. "We do admire it," said the overseer, affably. "But you shouldn't admire it," said the hunger artist. "Well then we don't admire it," said the overseer, "but why shouldn't we admire it?" "Because I have to fast, I can't help it," said the hunger artist. "What a fellow you are," said the overseer, "and why can't you help it?" "Because," said the hunger artist, lifting his head a little and speaking, with his lips pursed, as if for a kiss, right into the overseer's ear, so that no syllable might be lost, "because I couldn't find the food I liked. If I had found it, believe me, I should have made no fuss and stuffed myself like you or anyone else." These were his last words, but in his dimming eyes remained the firm though no longer proud persuasion that he was still continuing to fast.

"Well, clear this out now!" said the overseer, and they buried the hunger artist, straw and all. Into the cage they put a young panther. Even the most insensitive felt it refreshing to see this wild creature leaping around the cage that had so long been dreary. The panther was all right. The food he liked was brought him without hesitation by the attendants; he seemed not even to miss his freedom; his noble body, furnished almost to the bursting point with all that it needed, seemed to carry freedom around with it too; somewhere in his jaws it seemed to lurk; and the joy of life streamed with such ardent passion from his throat that for the onlookers it was not easy to stand the shock of it. But they braced themselves, crowded around the cage, and did not want ever to move away.

Interpretive Questions

1. Why does the hunger artist fail to find the audience he thinks he deserves?

2. Why is the hunger artist replaced by a young panther which immediately becomes a main attraction?

3. Why do people suspect the hunger artist is cheating at both the high and low points of his popularity?

4. In what sense was the hunger artist a "suffering martyr"?

5. Why does it turn out that the hunger artist fasted only because he never found the food he liked?

VIII

By and About John Locke

(1632–1704)

When John Locke was fifty-seven, he still had not published a word of his writings. Then, within four years, he published four works that brought him recognition in his lifetime and lasting fame as one of England's greatest philosophers: *A Letter Concerning Toleration, Two Treatises of Government, An Essay Concerning Human Understanding,* and *Some Thoughts Concerning Education.*

Locke said there are three faults that inhibit our thinking:

> The first is of those who seldom reason at all, but do and think according to the example of others . . . for the saving of themselves the pains and trouble of thinking and examining for themselves. The second is of those who put passion in the place of reason, . . . and these one may observe commonly content themselves with words, which have no distinct ideas to them, though in other matters that they come with an unbiased indifference to, they want not abilities to talk and hear reason. . . . The third sort is of those who readily and sincerely follow reason, but for want of having that which one may call large, sound, round-about sense have not a full view of all that relates to the question. . . . We are all short-sighted and often see but one side of a matter; our views are not extended to all that has a connection with it. From this defect I think no man is free.

He wrote about the difficulty of defining common terms:

> Any one almost would take it for an affront to be asked what he meant by [life]. And yet if it comes in question whether a plant that lies ready formed in the seed live, whether the embryo in an egg before incubation, or a man in a swoon without sense or motion be alive or no, it is easy to perceive that a clear, distinct, settled idea does not always accompany the use of so known a word as that of life is.

On doubting everything:

> If we will disbelieve everything because we cannot certainly know all things, we shall do muchwhat as wisely as he who would not use his legs, but sit still and perish because he had no wings to fly.

On education:

> The great skill of a teacher is to get and keep the attention of his scholar. . . . To attain this, he should make the child comprehend, as much as may be, the usefulness of what he teaches him and let him see, by what he has learned, that he can do something which gives him some power and real advantage over others who are ignorant of it.
>
> I confess there are some men's constitutions of body and mind so vigorous and well framed by nature that they need not much assistance from others, but by the strength of their natural genius they are from their cradles carried towards what is excellent, and by the privilege of their happy constitutions are able to do wonders. But examples of this kind are but few, and I think I may say that of all the men we meet with, nine parts of ten are what they are, good or evil, useful or not, by their education. 'Tis that which makes the great difference of mankind.

In Two Treatises on Government, *Locke states that any form of government is legitimate if it rests on the consent of the people and preserves their natural rights—that is, the rights they are born with. In our selection from the* Second Treatise, *he says that the first step people must take in establishing a new government is creating the legislative power. This power is bound by certain restrictions and obligations. The legislature must not delegate its authority; it must not raise taxes without the consent of the people; it must design all laws for the public good, publicize the laws, and apply them equally to the rich and the poor.*

A Letter Concerning Toleration argues that since matters of faith cannot be proved, people should be allowed to worship as they see fit. In our selection Locke maintains that a person is not obliged to obey a law that violates his conscience, and that a government ought not to enact such laws. When a government does, contending that the law is for the public good, and the individual refuses to obey it, declaring that the law is a bad one, God alone can judge—and will on Judgment Day. But, Locke asks, what shall be done in the meantime?

Of the Limits of Government

John Locke

The great end of men's entering into society being the enjoyment of their properties in peace and safety, and the great instrument and means of that being the laws established in that society, the first and fundamental positive law of all commonwealths is the establishing of the legislative power. . . . This legislative is not only the supreme power of the commonwealth, but sacred and unalterable in the hands where the community have once placed it; nor can any edict of anybody else, in what form soever conceived, or by what power soever backed, have the force and obligation of a law, which has not its sanction from that legislative which the public has chosen and appointed. For without this the law could not have that which is absolutely necessary to its being a law, the consent of the society over whom nobody can have a power to make laws, but by their own consent, and by authority received from them. . . .

---

*A selection from the *Second Treatise of Government* and *A Letter on Toleration*.

Though the legislative . . . be the supreme power in every commonwealth, yet,

First, it is not nor can possibly be absolutely arbitrary over the lives and fortunes of the people. For it being but the joint power of every member of the society given up to that person, or assembly, which is legislator, it can be no more than those persons had in a state of nature before they entered into society, and gave it up to the community. For nobody can transfer to another more power than he has in himself; and nobody has an absolute arbitrary power over himself, or over any other to destroy his own life, or take away the life or property of another. . . . [The legislative] power in the utmost bounds of it is limited to the public good of the society. It is a power that hath no other end but preservation, and therefore can never have a right to destroy, enslave, or designedly to impoverish the subjects. The obligations of the law of nature cease not in society, but only in many cases are drawn closer, and have by human laws known penalties annexed to them to enforce their observation. Thus the law of nature stands as an eternal rule to all men, legislators as well as others. The rules that they make for other men's actions must, as well as their own, and other men's actions, be comformable to the law of nature, i.e., to the will of God, of which that is a declaration, and the fundamental law of nature being the preservation of mankind, no human sanction can be good or valid against it.

Secondly, the legislative, or supreme authority, cannot assume to itself a power to rule by extemporary arbitrary decrees, but is bound to dispense justice, and decide the rights of the subject by promulgated standing laws, and known authorized judges. For the law of nature being unwritten, and so nowhere to be found but in the minds of men, they who through passion or interest shall miscite or misapply it cannot so easily be convinced of their mistake where there is no established judge. And so it serves not, as it ought, to determine the rights and fence the properties of those that live under it, especially where every one is judge, interpreter, and executioner of it too, and that in his own case; and he that has right on his side, having ordinarily but his own single strength, hath not force enough to defend himself from injuries or punish delinquents. To avoid these inconveniences, which disorder men's properties in the state of nature, men unite into societies that they may have the united strength of the whole society to secure and defend their properties and may have standing rules to bound it, by which every one may know what is his. To this end it is that men give up all their natural power to the society which they enter into, and the community put the legislative power into such hands as they think fit, with this trust, that they shall be governed by declared laws, or else their peace, quiet, and property will still be at the same uncertainty as it was in the state of nature. . . .

Thirdly, the supreme power cannot take from any man any part of his property without his own consent. For the preservation of property being the end of government, and that for which men enter into society, it necessarily supposes and requires that the people should have property, without which they must be supposed to lose that by entering into society, which was the end for which they entered into it, too gross an absurdity for any man to own. Men, therefore, in society having property, they have such a right to the goods which by the law of the community are theirs, that nobody hath a right to take them or any part of them from them, without their own consent; without this they have no property at all. For I have truly no property in that which another can by right take from me when he pleases, against my consent. Hence, it is a mistake to think that the supreme or legislative power of any commonwealth can do what it will, and dispose of the estates of the subjects arbitrarily, or take any part of them at pleasure. . . .

'Tis true governments cannot be supported without great

charge, and it is fit every one who enjoys a share of the protection should pay out of his estate his proportion for the maintenance of it. But still it must be with his own consent, i.e., the consent of the majority giving it either by themselves or their representatives chosen by them. For if any one shall claim a power to lay and levy taxes on the people by his own authority, and without such consent of the people, he thereby invades the fundamental law of property, and subverts the end of government. For what property have I in that which another may by right take when he pleases to himself?

Fourthly, the legislative cannot transfer the power of making laws to any other hands; for it being but a delegated power from the people, they who have it cannot pass it over to others. The people alone can appoint the form of the commonwealth, which is by constituting the legislative, and appointing in whose hands that shall be. And when the people have said we will submit to rules, and be governed by laws made by such men, and in such forms, nobody else can say other men shall make laws for them; nor can the people be bound by any laws but such as are enacted by those whom they have chosen and authorized to make laws for them.

These are the bounds which the trust that is put in them by the society, and the law of God and Nature, have set to the legislative power of every commonwealth, in all forms of government.

First, they are to govern by promulgated established laws, not to be varied in particular cases, but to have one rule for rich and poor, for the favorite at court and the countryman at plow.

Secondly, these laws also ought to be designed for no other end ultimately but the good of the people.

Thirdly, they must not raise taxes on the property of people without the consent of the people, given by themselves or their deputies. And this properly concerns only such governments where the legislative is always in being, or at least where the people have not reserved any part of the legislative to deputies, to be from time to time chosen by themselves.

Fourthly, the legislative neither must nor can transfer the power of making laws to anybody else, or place it anywhere but where the people have.

A Letter on Toleration

It is easy to understand to what end the legislative power ought to be directed, and by what measures regulated; and that is the temporal good and outward prosperity of the society, which is the sole reason of men's entering into society, and the only thing they seek and aim at in it. And it is also evident what liberty remains to men in reference to their eternal salvation, and that is, that every one should do what he in his conscience is persuaded to be acceptable to the Almighty, on whose good pleasure and acceptance depends his eternal happiness; for obedience is due in the first place to God, and afterwards to the laws.

But some may ask, "What if the magistrate should enjoin anything by his authority that appears unlawful to the conscience of a private person?" I answer that if government be faithfully administered, and the counsels of the magistrate be indeed directed to the public good, this will seldom happen. But if perhaps it do so fall out, I say that such a private person is to abstain from the actions that he judges unlawful, and he is to undergo the punishment, which is not unlawful for him to bear; for the private judgment of any person concerning a law enacted in political matters, for the public good, does not take away the obligation of that law, nor deserve a dispensation. But if the law indeed be concerning things that lie not within the verge of the magistrate's authority (as, for example,

that the people, or any party amongst them, should be compelled to embrace a strange religion, and join in the worship
and ceremonies of another church), men are not in these cases
obliged by that law, against their consciences; for the political
society is instituted for no other end, but only to secure every
man's possession of the things of this life. The care of each
man's soul, and of the things of heaven, which neither does
belong to the commonwealth nor can be subjected to it, is left
entirely to every man's self. Thus the safeguard of men's lives,
and of the things that belong unto this life, is the business of
the commonwealth; and the preserving of those things unto
their owners is the duty of the magistrate. And therefore the
magistrate cannot take away these worldly things from this
man, or party, and give them to that; nor change property
amongst fellow-subjects, no not even by a law, for a cause that
has no relation to the end of civil government: I mean for their
religion, which, whether it be true or false, does no prejudice
to the worldly concerns of their fellow-subjects, which are the
things that only belong unto the care of the commonwealth.

"But what if the magistrate believe such a law as this to be
for the public good?" I answer: as the private judgment of any
particular person, if erroneous, does not exempt him from the
obligation of law, so the private judgment, as I may call it, of
the magistrate does not give him any new right of imposing
laws upon his subjects, which neither was in the constitution
of the government granted him, nor ever was in the power of
the people to grant, and least of all, if he make it his business
to enrich and advance his followers and fellow-sectaries with
the spoils of others. But what if the magistrate believe that he
has a right to make such laws, and that they are for the public
good; and his subjects believe the contrary? Who shall be judge
between them? I answer, God alone; for there is no judge upon
earth between the supreme magistrate and the people. God,
I say, is the only judge in this case, who will retribute unto

every one at the last day according to his deserts; that is, according to his sincerity and uprightness in endeavoring to promote piety, and the public weal and peace of mankind. But what shall be done in the meanwhile? I answer: the principal and chief care of every one ought to be of his own soul first, and, in the next place, of the public peace: though yet there are few will think it is peace there, where they see all laid waste. There are two sorts of contests amongst men, the one managed by law, the other by force: and they are of that nature, that where the one ends, the other always begins. But it is not my business to inquire into the power of the magistrate in the different constitutions of nations. I only know what usually happens where controversies arise without a judge to determine them. You will say then the magistrate being the stronger will have his will and carry his point. Without doubt. But the question is not here concerning the doubtfulness of the event, but the rule of right.

▮▮

Interpretive Questions

1. Could Locke's conception of government cover anything from a hereditary monarchy to a democracy?

2. Does Locke offer any incentive for people without property to enter into a political society?

3. Is the magistrate who attempts to enforce a bad law immune from punishment, according to Locke?

4. Does a person have an obligation *not* to obey a law that violates his conscience?

5. Do the people have any control over the legislature once they have formed it? What check does natural law have on the legislature?

According to Aris†
be happy without

Why can we only
replacing it wit

What does Mother r
Father Hugh has a
rejects it?

s Socrates conce
ntegrity or with t

Why does Mil
ultimate appe

Is someone who
laws likely to h

Is the hunger artist

Why does Locke r
property, rather
and liberty, the

At what point
about his edict

Why are people contin
democratic society?

Does Woolf thin
magnifying mirro

Why does the pho
and make him ho

Why don't the

Developing Interpretive Questions

The more you participate in Great Books discussions, the more you will see problems of meaning in the selections you read. Some of your notes may already be in the form of interpretive questions; others can be developed into questions.

Writing interpretive questions from your notes will help you to prepare for discussion. Remember that an interpretive question is a question you care about that can be explored using the text everyone has read. It has more than one possible correct answer.

The most likely sources of interpretive questions are listed here, together with the questions one reader developed from her responses to "A Letter on Toleration."

What seems important. Locke says that because neither a person's soul nor the things of heaven can be subjected to the commonwealth, a person is not bound by a law that violates his conscience. The reader wanted to know if Locke thought a citizen should accept the consequences of disobeying such a law. She wrote this question:

> Should an individual submit to punishment for disobeying any law that violates personal conscience, according to Locke?

What you don't understand. The reader did not understand Locke's explanation regarding a magistrate who tries to enforce a bad law. She was unsure of whether the magistrate could be punished, so she asked this question:

> Is the magistrate who attempts to enforce a bad law immune to punishment?

What you agree or disagree with. The reader disagreed with Locke's statement that the political society is instituted "for no other end, but only to secure every man's possession of the things of this life." She reasoned that if this were the case, an individual without possessions would never enter into such a society. This question came out of her disagreement with Locke's assertion:

> Does Locke offer an incentive for people without property to enter into a political society?

What the author seems to emphasize. Locke places great emphasis on individual conscience. The reader therefore wondered what a person ought to do if a law that violates his or her conscience is enacted. She asked this question:

> Does a person have an obligation not to obey a law that violates his or her conscience?

IX

About the Oedipus Plays of Sophocles

Oedipus the King, Oedipus at Colonus, and *Antigone,* Sophocles' best-known plays, dramatize the ancient legend of Oedipus, King of Thebes, and his family.

As a young man, Oedipus learned from the Delphic oracle that he would kill his father and marry his mother, so he left his home in Corinth to escape his fate. During his travels he killed a stranger in a quarrel. Later he became a hero by solving the riddle of the sphinx and thereby rescuing the city of Thebes from her power. For this he was rewarded with marriage to Jocasta, the recently-widowed queen. They had four children: Eteocles, Polyneices, Ismene, and Antigone.

As *Oedipus the King* opens, Thebes is being destroyed by a plague because King Laius' murderer has not been punished. Oedipus vows to bring the man to justice and then, through a series of painful revelations, learns that he is the man. As he discovers what he has done, Oedipus also learns who he is: the son of Laius and Jocasta, left to die as an infant because he was fated to kill his father. As the play ends, Jocasta commits suicide and Oedipus puts out his eyes and banishes himself from Thebes. The chorus, which sometimes acts as a composite character and sometimes as the voice of public opinion, comments:

> Oedipus seemed blessed, but there is no man blessed amongst men. . . . Time watches, he is eagle-eyed. And all the works of man are known and every soul is tried.

Oedipus at Colonus is about the end of Oedipus' life. As an old man he arrives at the grove of the Eumenidies, outside Athens, to die. Because an oracle has promised that Oedipus will be a blessing to the city that buries him and a curse to the one that casts him out, Creon, who is acting ruler of Thebes, and Theseus, ruler of Athens, both offer him sanctuary. He accepts Theseus' offer.

An outcast who has spent his life wandering about with his daughters Antigone and Ismene, Oedipus is bitter about his fate. He insists that he is blameless because he sinned in ignorance. He is also enraged with his two sons, who have permitted him to spend his entire life in exile. He curses them both and predicts that they will slay one another in their battle for the throne of Thebes.

Just before he dies, Oedipus takes leave of his daughters and walks away with Theseus to a predestined place. A messenger reports that "he was taken ... without grief or agony — a passing more wonderful than that of any other man."

Theseus offers to return Antigone and Ismene to Thebes and, as *Antigone* opens, Oedipus' prophecy has just proved true: Eteocles and Polyneices have killed each other outside the gates of Thebes. Creon has proclaimed an edict forbidding proper burial of Polyneices.

THE CHARACTERS

ANTIGONE ⎫
⎬ *daughters of Oedipus*
ISMENE ⎭

CREON, *King of Thebes*

EURYDICE, *his wife*

HAIMON, *his son*

TEIRESIAS, *the blind prophet*

A SENTRY

A MESSENGER

CHORUS, *citizens of Thebes*

CHORAGOS, *leader of the* CHORUS

Antigone

Sophocles

SCENE: Before the Palace of CREON, *King of Thebes. A central double door, and two lateral doors. A platform extends the length of the facade, and from this platform three steps lead down into the orchestra, or chorus-ground. Time: dawn of the day after the repulse of the Argive army from the assault on Thebes.*

PROLOGUE

[ANTIGONE *and* ISMENE *enter from the central door of the Palace.*]

ANTIGONE: Ismene, dear sister,
   You would think that we have already suffered enough
   For the curse on Oedipus:
   I cannot imagine any grief
   That you and I have not gone through. And now—
   Have they told you the new decree of our King Creon?

ISMENE: I have heard nothing: I know
That two sisters lost two brothers, a double death
In a single hour; and I know that the Argive army
Fled in the night; but beyond this, nothing.

ANTIGONE: I thought so. And that is why I wanted you
To come out here with me. There is something we
    must do.

ISMENE: Why do you speak so strangely?

ANTIGONE: Listen, Ismene:
Creon buried our brother Eteocles
With military honors, gave him a soldier's funeral,
And it was right that he should; but Polyneices,
Who fought as bravely and died as miserably,—
They say that Creon has sworn
No one shall bury him, no one mourn for him,
But his body must lie in the fields, a sweet treasure
For carrion birds to find as they search for food.
That is what they say, and our good Creon is coming
    here
To announce it publicly; and the penalty—
Stoning to death in the public square!
                              There it is,
And now you can prove what you are:
A true sister, or a traitor to your family.

ISMENE: Antigone, you are mad! What could I possibly do?

ANTIGONE: You must decide whether you will help me or
not.

ISMENE: I do not understand you. Help you in what?

ANTIGONE: Ismene, I am going to bury him. Will you
come?

ISMENE: Bury him! You have just said the new law forbids
it.

ANTIGONE: He is my brother. And he is your brother, too.

ISMENE: But think of the danger! Think what Creon will
do!

ANTIGONE: Creon is not strong enough to stand in my
way.

ISMENE: Ah sister!
Oedipus died, everyone hating him
For what his own search brought to light, his eyes
Ripped out by his own hand; and Iocaste died,
His mother and wife at once: she twisted the cords
That strangled her life; and our two brothers died,
Each killed by the other's sword. And we are left:
But oh, Antigone,
Think how much more terrible than these
Our own death would be if we should go against Creon
And do what he has forbidden! We are only women,
We cannot fight with men, Antigone!
The law is strong, we must give in to the law
In this thing, and in worse. I beg the Dead
To forgive me, but I am helpless: I must yield
To those in authority. And I think it is dangerous
business
To be always meddling.

ANTIGONE: If that is what you think,
I should not want you, even if you asked to come.
You have made your choice, you can be what you want
to be.
But I will bury him; and if I must die,

I say that this crime is holy: I shall lie down
With him in death, and I shall be as dear
To him as he to me.
                              It is the dead,
Not the living, who make the longest demands:
We die forever ...
                              You may do as you like,
Since apparently the laws of the gods mean nothing
    to you.

ISMENE: They mean a great deal to me; but I have no
    strength
To break laws that were made for the public good.

ANTIGONE: That must be your excuse, I suppose. But as
    for me,
I will bury the brother I love.

ISMENE: Antigone,
I am so afraid for you!

ANTIGONE: You need not be:
You have yourself to consider, after all.

ISMENE: But no one must hear of this, you must tell no
    one!
I will keep it a secret, I promise!

ANTIGONE: Oh tell it! Tell everyone!
Think how they'll hate you when it all comes out
If they learn that you knew about it all the time!

ISMENE: So fiery! You should be cold with fear.

ANTIGONE: Perhaps. But I am doing only what I must.

ISMENE: But can you do it? I say that you cannot.

ANTIGONE: Very well: when my strength gives out, I shall
do no more.

ISMENE: Impossible things should not be tried at all.

ANTIGONE: Go away, Ismene:
I shall be hating you soon, and the dead will too,
For your words are hateful. Leave me my foolish plan:
I am not afraid of the danger; if it means death,
It will not be the worst of deaths—death without honor.

ISMENE: Go then, if you feel that you must.
You are unwise,
But a loyal friend indeed to those who love you.

[*Exit into the Palace.* ANTIGONE *goes off. Enter the*
CHORUS.]

PARODOS

CHORUS: Now the long blade of the sun, lying
Level east to west, touches with glory
Thebes of the Seven Gates. Open, unlidded
Eye of golden day! O marching light
Across the eddy and rush of Dirce's stream,
Striking the white shields of the enemy
Thrown headlong backward from the blaze of morning!

CHORAGOS: Polyneices their commander
Roused them with windy phrases,
He the wild eagle screaming
Insults above our land,
His wings their shields of snow,
His crest their marshalled helms.

CHORUS: Against our seven gates in a yawning ring
    The famished spears came onward in the night;
    But before his jaws were sated with our blood,
    Or pinefire took the garland of our towers,
    He was thrown back; and as he turned, great Thebes—
    No tender victim for his noisy power—
    Rose like a dragon behind him, shouting war.

CHORAGOS: For God hates utterly
    The bray of bragging tongues;
    And when he beheld their smiling,
    Their swagger of golden helms,
    The frown of his thunder blasted
    Their first man from our walls.

CHORUS: We heard his shout of triumph high in the air
    Turn to a scream; far out in a flaming arc
    He fell with his windy torch, and the earth struck him.
    And others storming in fury no less than his
    Found shock of death in the dusty joy of battle.

CHORAGOS: Seven captains at seven gates
    Yielded their clanging arms to the god
    That bends the battle-line and breaks it.
    These two only, brothers in blood,
    Face to face in matchless rage,
    Mirroring each the other's death,
    Clashed in long combat.

CHORUS: But now in the beautiful morning of victory
    Let Thebes of the many chariots sing for joy!
    With hearts for dancing we'll take leave of war:
    Our temples shall be sweet with hymns of praise,
    And the long night shall echo with our chorus.

SCENE I

CHORAGOS: But now at last our new King is coming:
Creon of Thebes, Menoiceus' son.
In this auspicious dawn of his reign
What are the new complexities
That shifting Fate has woven for him?
What is his counsel? Why has he summoned
The old men to hear him?

> [*Enter* CREON *from the Palace. He addresses the*
> CHORUS *from the top step.*]

CREON: Gentlemen: I have the honor to inform you that our
Ship of State, which recent storms have threatened to
destroy, has come safely to harbor at last, guided by the
merciful wisdom of Heaven. I have summoned you here this
morning because I know that I can depend upon you: your
devotion to King Laios was absolute; you never hesitated in
your duty to our late ruler Oedipus; and when Oedipus died,
your loyalty was transferred to his children. Unfortunately,
as you know, his two sons, the princes Eteocles and
Polyneices, have killed each other in battle; and I, as the
next in blood, have succeeded to the full power of the
throne.

I am aware, of course, that no Ruler can expect complete
loyalty from his subjects until he has been tested in office.
Nevertheless, I say to you at the very outset that I have
nothing but contempt for the kind of Governor who is
afraid, for whatever reason, to follow the course that he
knows is best for the State; and as for the man who sets
private friendship above the public welfare,—I have no use
for him, either. I call God to witness that if I saw my country
headed for ruin, I should not be afraid to speak out plainly;

and I need hardly remind you that I would never have any dealings with an enemy of the people. No one values friendship more highly than I; but we must remember that friends made at the risk of wrecking our Ship are not real friends at all.

These are my principles, at any rate, and that is why I have made the following decision concerning the sons of Oedipus: Eteocles, who died as a man should die, fighting for his country, is to be buried with full military honors, with all the ceremony that is usual when the greatest heroes die; but his brother Polyneices, who broke his exile to come back with fire and sword against his native city and the shrines of his fathers' gods, whose own idea was to spill the blood of his blood and sell his own people into slavery—Polyneices, I say, is to have no burial: no man is to touch him or say the least prayer for him; he shall lie on the plain, unburied; and the birds and the scavenging dogs can do with him whatever they like.

This is my command, and you can see the wisdom behind it. As long as I am King, no traitor is going to be honored with the loyal man. But whoever shows by word and deed that he is on the side of the State,—he shall have my respect while he is living, and my reverence when he is dead.

CHORAGOS: If that is your will, Creon son of Menoiceus,
You have the right to enforce it: we are yours.

CREON: That is my will. Take care that you do your part.

CHORAGOS: We are old men: let the younger ones carry it out.

CREON: I do not mean that: the sentries have been appointed.

CHORAGOS: Then what is it that you would have us do?

CREON: You will give no support to whoever breaks this law.

CHORAGOS: Only a crazy man is in love with death!

CREON: And death it is: yet money talks, and the wisest
Have sometimes been known to count a few coins too
many.

[*Enter* SENTRY.]

SENTRY: I'll not say that I'm out of breath from running,
King, because every time I stopped to think about what I
have to tell you, I felt like going back. And all the time a
voice kept saying, "You fool, don't you know you're walking
straight into trouble?"; and then another voice: "Yes, but if
you let somebody else get the news to Creon first, it will be
even worse than that for you!" But good sense won out, at
least I hope it was good sense, and here I am with a story that
makes no sense at all; but I'll tell it anyhow, because, as they
say, what's going to happen's going to happen, and—

CREON: Come to the point. What have you to say?

SENTRY: I did not do it. I did not see who did it. You must
not punish me for what someone else has done.

CREON: A comprehensive defense! More effective, perhaps,
If I knew its purpose. Come: what is it?

SENTRY: A dreadful thing ... I don't know how to put
it—

CREON: Out with it!

SENTRY: Well, then;
The dead man—
                   Polyneices—
                              out there—
                                        someone,—

New dust on the slimy flesh!
Someone has given it burial that way, and
Gone . . .

CREON: And the man who dared do this?

SENTRY: I swear I
Do not know! You must believe me!
                                    Listen:
The ground was dry, not a sign of digging, no,
Not a wheeltrack in the dust, no trace of anyone.
It was when they relieved us this morning: and one of
    them,
The corporal, pointed to it.
                            There it was,
The strangest—
                    Look:
The body, just mounded over there with light dust: you
    see?
Not buried really, but as if they'd covered it
Just enough for the ghost's peace. And no sign
Of dogs or any wild animal that had been there.

And then what a scene there was! Every man of us
Accusing the other: we all proved the other man did it,
We all had proof that we could not have done it.
We were ready to take hot iron in our hands,
Walk through fire, swear by all the gods,
It was not I!
I do not know who it was, but it was not I!
And then, when this came to nothing, someone said
A thing that silenced us and made us stare
Down at the ground: you had to be told the news,
And one of us had to do it! We threw the dice,

And the bad luck fell to me. So here I am,
No happier to be here than you are to have me:
Nobody likes the man who brings bad news.

CHORAGOS: I have been wondering, King: can it be that the
gods have done this?

CREON: Stop!
Must you doddering wrecks
Go out of your heads entirely? "The gods!"
Intolerable!
The gods favor this corpse? Why? How had he served
   them?
Tried to loot their temples, burn their images,
Yes, and the whole State, and its laws with it!
Is it your senile opinion that the gods love to honor bad
   men?
A pious thought!—
                    No, from the very beginning
There have been those who have whispered together,
Stiff-necked anarchists, putting their heads together,
Scheming against me in alleys. These are the men,
And they have bribed my own guard to do this thing.

Money!
There's nothing in the world so demoralizing as money.
Down go your cities,
Homes gone, men gone, honest hearts corrupted,
Crookedness of all kinds, and all for money!

                              [to SENTRY]   But you—!
I swear by God and by the throne of God,
The man who has done this thing shall pay for it!
Find that man, bring him here to me, or your death
Will be the least of your problems: I'll string you up

Alive, and there will be certain ways to make you
Discover your employer before you die;
And the process may teach you a lesson you seem to have
  missed:
The dearest profit is sometimes all too dear:
That depends on the source. Do you understand me?
A fortune won is often misfortune.

SENTRY: King, may I speak?

CREON: Your very voice distresses me.

SENTRY: Are you sure that it is my voice, and not your
conscience?

CREON: By God, he wants to analyze me now!

SENTRY: It is not what I say, but what has been done, that
hurts you.

CREON: You talk too much.

SENTRY: Maybe; but I've done nothing.

CREON: Sold your soul for some silver; that's all you've
done.

SENTRY: How dreadful it is when the right judge judges
wrong!

CREON: Your figures of speech
May entertain you now; but unless you bring me the
  man,
You will get little profit from them in the end.

                            [*Exit* CREON *into the Palace.*]

SENTRY: "Bring me the man"—!
I'd like nothing better than bringing him the man!

But bring him or not, you have seen the last of me here.
At any rate, I am safe!

[*Exit* SENTRY.]

ODE I

CHORUS: Numberless are the world's wonders, but none
More wonderful than man; the stormgray sea
Yields to his prows, the huge crests bear him high;
Earth, holy and inexhaustible, is graven
With shining furrows where his plows have gone
Year after year, the timeless labor of stallions.

The lightboned birds and beasts that cling to cover,
The lithe fish lighting their reaches of dim water,
All are taken, tamed in the net of his mind;
The lion on the hill, the wild horse windy-maned,
Resign to him; and his blunt yoke has broken
The sultry shoulders of the mountain bull.

Words also, and thought as rapid as air,
He fashions to his good use; statecraft is his,
And his the skill that deflects the arrows of snow,
The spears of winter rain: from every wind
He has made himself secure—from all but one:
In the late wind of death he cannot stand.

O clear intelligence, force beyond all measure!
O fate of man, working both good and evil!
When the laws are kept, how proudly his city stands!
When the laws are broken, what of his city then?

Never may the anarchic man find rest at my hearth,
Never be it said that my thoughts are his thoughts.

SCENE II

[*Re-enter* SENTRY *leading* ANTIGONE.]

CHORAGOS: What does this mean? Surely this captive
    woman
Is the Princess, Antigone. Why should she be taken?

SENTRY: Here is the one who did it! We caught her
In the very act of burying him.—Where is Creon?

CHORAGOS: Just coming from the house.

[*Enter* CREON.]

CREON: What has happened?
    Why have you come back so soon?

SENTRY: O King,
    A man should never be too sure of anything:
    I would have sworn
    That you'd not see me here again: your anger
    Frightened me so, and the things you threatened me
        with;
    But how could I tell then
    That I'd be able to solve the case so soon?

    No dice-throwing this time: I was only too glad to come!

    Here is this woman. She is the guilty one:
    We found her trying to bury him.

Take her, then; question her; judge her as you will.
I am through with the whole thing now, and glad of it.

CREON: But this is Antigone! Why have you brought her here?

SENTRY: She was burying him, I tell you!

CREON: Is this the truth?

SENTRY: I saw her with my own eyes. Can I say more?

CREON: The details: come, tell me quickly!

SENTRY: It was like this:
After those terrible threats of yours, King,
We went back and brushed the dust away from the body.
The flesh was soft by now, and stinking,
So we sat on a hill to windward and kept guard.
No napping this time! We kept each other awake.
But nothing happened until the white round sun
Whirled in the center of the round sky over us:
Then, suddenly,
A storm of dust roared up from the earth, and the sky
Went out, the plain vanished with all its trees
In the stinging dark. We closed our eyes and endured it.
The whirlwind lasted a long time, but it passed;
And then we looked, and there was Antigone!
I have seen
A mother bird come back to a stripped nest, heard
Her crying bitterly a broken note or two
For the young ones stolen. Just so, when this girl
Found the bare corpse, and all her love's work wasted,
She wept, and cried on heaven to damn the hands

That had done this thing.
And then she brought more dust
And sprinkled wine three times for her brother's ghost.

We ran and took her at once. She was not afraid,
Not even when we charged her with what she had done.
She denied nothing.
And this was a comfort to me,
And some uneasiness: for it is a good thing
To escape from death, but it is no great pleasure
To bring death to a friend.
Yet I always say
There is nothing so comfortable as your own safe skin!

CREON: And you, Antigone,
You with your head hanging—do you confess this thing?

ANTIGONE: I do. I deny nothing.

CREON: [*to* SENTRY]
You may go.
[*Exit* SENTRY.]

[*to* ANTIGONE]

Tell me, tell me briefly:
Had you heard my proclamation touching this matter?

ANTIGONE: It was public. Could I help hearing it?

CREON: And yet you dared defy the law.

ANTIGONE:
I dared.
It was not God's proclamation. That final Justice
That rules the world below makes no such laws.

Your edict, King, was strong,
But all your strength is weakness itself against

The immortal unrecorded laws of God.
They are not merely now: they were, and shall be,
Operative forever, beyond man utterly.

I knew I must die, even without your decree:
I am only mortal. And if I must die
Now, before it is my time to die,
Surely this is no hardship: can anyone
Living, as I live, with evil all about me,
Think Death less than a friend? This death of mine
Is of no importance; but if I had left my brother
Lying in death unburied, I should have suffered.
Now I do not.
                    You smile at me. Ah Creon,
Think me a fool, if you like; but it may well be
That a fool convicts me of folly.

CHORAGOS: Like father, like daughter: both headstrong,
      deaf to reason!
She has never learned to yield.

CREON: She has much to learn.
    The inflexible heart breaks first, the toughest iron
    Cracks first, and the wildest horses bend their necks
    At the pull of the smallest curb.
                              Pride? In a slave?
    This girl is guilty of a double insolence,
    Breaking the given laws and boasting of it.
    Who is the man here,
    She or I, if this crime goes unpunished?
    Sister's child, or more than sister's child,
    Or closer yet in blood—she and her sister
    Win bitter death for this!

[*to* SERVANTS]   Go, some of you,
 Arrest Ismene. I accuse her equally.
 Bring her: you will find her sniffling in the house there.
 Her mind's a traitor: crimes kept in the dark
 Cry for light, and the guardian brain shudders;
 But how much worse than this
 Is brazen boasting of barefaced anarchy!

ANTIGONE: Creon, what more do you want than my
 death?

CREON   Nothing.
 That gives me everything.

ANTIGONE: Then I beg you: kill me.
 This talking is a great weariness: your words
 Are distasteful to me, and I am sure that mine
 Seem so to you. And yet they should not seem so:
 I should have praise and honor for what I have done.
 All these men here would praise me
 Were their lips not frozen shut with fear of you.
 Ah the good fortune of kings,
 Licensed to say and do whatever they please!

CREON: You are alone here in that opinion.

ANTIGONE: No, they are with me. But they keep their
 tongues in leash.

CREON: Maybe. But you are guilty, and they are not.

ANTIGONE: There is no guilt in reverence for the dead.

CREON: But Eteocles—was he not your brother too?

ANTIGONE: My brother too.

CREON: And you insult his memory?

ANTIGONE: The dead man would not say that I insult it.

CREON: He would: for you honor a traitor as much as him.

ANTIGONE: His own brother, traitor or not, and equal in blood.

CREON: He made war on his country. Eteocles defended it.

ANTIGONE: Nevertheless, there are honors due all the dead.

CREON: But not the same for the wicked as for the just.

ANTIGONE: Ah Creon, Creon,
Which of us can say what the gods hold wicked?

CREON: An enemy is an enemy, even dead.

ANTIGONE: It is my nature to join in love, not hate.

CREON: Go join them, then; if you must have your love,
Find it in hell!

CHORAGOS: But see, Ismene comes:

[*Enter* ISMENE, *guarded.*]
Those tears are sisterly, the cloud
That shadows her eyes rains down gentle sorrow.

CREON: You too, Ismene,
Snake in my ordered house, sucking my blood
Stealthily—and all the time I never knew
That these two sisters were aiming at my throne!

Ismene,

Do you confess your share in this crime, or deny it?
Answer me.

ISMENE: Yes, if she will let me say so. I am guilty.

ANTIGONE: No, Ismene. You have no right to say so.
You would not help me, and I will not have you help me.

ISMENE: But now I know what you meant; and I am here
To join you, to take my share of punishment.

ANTIGONE: The dead man and the gods who rule the dead
Know whose act this was. Words are not friends.

ISMENE: Do you refuse me, Antigone? I want to die with you:
I too have a duty that I must discharge to the dead.

ANTIGONE: You shall not lessen my death by sharing it.

ISMENE: What do I care for life when you are dead?

ANTIGONE: Ask Creon. You're always hanging on his opinions.

ISMENE: You are laughing at me. Why, Antigone?

ANTIGONE: It's a joyless laughter, Ismene.

ISMENE: But can I do nothing?

ANTIGONE: Yes. Save yourself. I shall not envy you.
There are those who will praise you; I shall have honor, too.

ISMENE: But we are equally guilty!

ANTIGONE: No more, Ismene.
You are alive, but I belong to Death.

CREON: [*to the* CHORUS]
  Gentlemen, I beg you to observe these girls:
  One has just now lost her mind; the other,
  It seems, has never had a mind at all.

ISMENE: Grief teaches the steadiest minds to waver, King.

CREON: Yours certainly did, when you assumed guilt with
  the guilty!

ISMENE: But how could I go on living without her?

CREON: You are.
  She is already dead.

ISMENE: But your own son's bride!

CREON: There are places enough for him to push his
  plow.
  I want no wicked women for my sons!

ISMENE: O dearest Haimon, how your father wrongs you!

CREON: I've had enough of your childish talk of marriage!

CHORAGOS: Do you really intend to steal this girl from your
  son?

CREON: No; Death will do that for me.

CHORAGOS: Then she must die?

CREON: You dazzle me.
                      —But enough of this talk!
  [*to* GUARDS]
  You, there, take them away and guard them well:
  For they are but women, and even brave men run
  When they see Death coming.

                      [*Exeunt* ISMENE, ANTIGONE, *and* GUARDS.]

ODE II

CHORUS: Fortunate is the man who has never tasted God's
    vengeance!
  Where once the anger of heaven has struck, that house
    is shaken
  Forever: damnation rises behind each child
  Like a wave cresting out of the black northeast,
  When the long darkness under sea roars up
  And bursts drumming death upon the windwhipped sand.

  I have seen this gathering sorrow from time long past
  Loom upon Oedipus' children: generation from
    generation
  Takes the compulsive rage of the enemy god.
  So lately this last flower of Oedipus' line
  Drank the sunlight! but now a passionate word
  And a handful of dust have closed up all its beauty.

    What mortal arrogance
    Transcends the wrath of Zeus?
  Sleep cannot lull him, nor the effortless long months
  Of the timeless gods: but he is young forever,
  And his house is the shining day of high Olympos.
    All that is and shall be,
    And all the past, is his.
  No pride on earth is free of the curse of heaven.

    The straying dreams of men
    May bring them ghosts of joy:
  But as they drowse, the waking embers burn them;
  Or they walk with fixed eyes, as blind men walk.
  But the ancient wisdom speaks for our own time:

Fate works most for woe
With Folly's fairest show.
Man's little pleasure is the spring of sorrow.

SCENE III

CHORAGOS: But here is Haimon, King, the last of all your
sons.
Is it grief for Antigone that brings him here,
And bitterness at being robbed of his bride?

[*Enter* HAIMON.]

CREON: We shall soon see, and no need of diviners.
—Son,
You have heard my final judgment on that girl:
Have you come here hating me, or have you come
With deference and with love, whatever I do?

HAIMON: I am your son, father. You are my guide.
You make things clear for me, and I obey you.
No marriage means more to me than your continuing
wisdom.

CREON: Good. That is the way to behave: subordinate
Everything else, my son, to your father's will.
This is what a man prays for, that he may get
Sons attentive and dutiful in his house,
Each one hating his father's enemies,
Honoring his father's friends. But if his sons
Fail him, if they turn out unprofitably,
What has he fathered but trouble for himself
And amusement for the malicious?
So you are right

Not to lose your head over this woman.
Your pleasure with her would soon grow cold, Haimon,
And then you'd have a hellcat in bed and elsewhere.
Let her find her husband in Hell!
Of all the people in this city, only she
Has had contempt for my law and broken it.

Do you want me to show myself weak before the people?
Or to break my sworn word? No, and I will not.
The woman dies.

I suppose she'll plead "family ties." Well, let her.
If I permit my own family to rebel,
How shall I earn the world's obedience?
Show me the man who keeps his house in hand,
He's fit for public authority.
                              I'll have no dealings
With law-breakers, critics of the government:
Whoever is chosen to govern should be obeyed—
Must be obeyed, in all things, great and small,
Just and unjust! O Haimon,
The man who knows how to obey, and that man only,
Knows how to give commands when the time comes.
You can depend on him, no matter how fast
The spears come: he's a good soldier, he'll stick it out.

Anarchy, anarchy! Show me a greater evil!
This is why cities tumble and the great houses rain down,
This is what scatters armies!

No, no: good lives are made so by discipline.
We keep the laws then, and the lawmakers,
And no woman shall seduce us. If we must lose,

Let's lose to a man, at least! Is a woman stronger than
  we?

CHORAGOS: Unless time has rusted my wits,
  What you say, King, is said with point and dignity.

HAIMON: Father:
  Reason is God's crowning gift to man, and you are right
  To warn me against losing mine. I cannot say—
  I hope that I shall never want to say!—that you
  Have reasoned badly. Yet there are other men
  Who can reason, too; and their opinions might be helpful.
  You are not in a position to know everything
  That people say or do, or what they feel:
  Your temper terrifies them—everyone
  Will tell you only what you like to hear.
  But I, at any rate, can listen; and I have heard them
  Muttering and whispering in the dark about this girl.
  They say no woman has ever, so unreasonably,
  Died so shameful a death for a generous act:
  "She covered her brother's body. Is this indecent?
  She kept him from dogs and vultures. Is this a crime?
  Death?—She should have all the honor that we can give
    her!"

This is the way they talk out there in the city.

You must believe me:
Nothing is closer to me than your happiness.
What could be closer? Must not any son
Value his father's fortune as his father does his?
I beg you, do not be unchangeable:
Do not believe that you alone can be right.
The man who thinks that,

The man who maintains that only he has the power
To reason correctly, the gift to speak, the soul—
A man like that, when you know him, turns out empty.

It is not reason never to yield to reason!

In flood time you can see how some trees bend,
And because they bend, even their twigs are safe,
While stubborn trees are torn up, roots and all.
And the same thing happens in sailing:
Make your sheet fast, never slacken,—and over you go.
Head over heels and under: and there's your voyage.
Forget you are angry! Let yourself be moved!
I know I am young; but please let me say this:
The ideal condition
Would be, I admit, that men should be right by instinct;
But since we are all too likely to go astray,
The reasonable thing is to learn from those who can
    teach.

CHORAGOS: You will do well to listen to him, King,
    If what he says is sensible. And you, Haimon,
    Must listen to your father.—Both speak well.

CREON: You consider it right for a man of my years and
    experience
    To go to school to a boy?

HAIMON: It is not right
    If I am wrong. But if I am young, and right,
    What does my age matter?

CREON: You think it right to stand up for an anarchist?

HAIMON: Not at all. I pay no respect to criminals.

CREON: Then she is not a criminal?

HAIMON: The City would deny it, to a man.

CREON: And the City proposes to teach me how to rule?

HAIMON: Ah. Who is it that's talking like a boy now?

CREON: My voice is the one voice giving orders in this City!

HAIMON: It is no City if it takes orders from one voice.

CREON: The State is the King!

HAIMON: Yes, if the State is a desert.

CREON: This boy, it seems, has sold out to a woman.

HAIMON: If you are a woman: my concern is only for you.

CREON: So? Your "concern"! In a public brawl with your father!

HAIMON: How about you, in a public brawl with justice?

CREON: With justice, when all that I do is within my rights?

HAIMON: You have no right to trample on God's right.

CREON: Fool, adolescent fool! Taken in by a woman!

HAIMON: You'll never see me taken in by anything vile.

CREON: Every word you say is for her!

HAIMON: And for you.
And for me. And for the gods under the earth.

CREON: You'll never marry her while she lives.

HAIMON: Then she must die.—But her death will cause another.

CREON: Another?
Have you lost your senses? Is this an open threat?

HAIMON: There is no threat in speaking to emptiness.

CREON: I swear you'll regret this superior tone of yours!
You are the empty one!

HAIMON: If you were not my father,
I'd say you were perverse.

CREON: You girlstruck fool, don't play at words with me!

HAIMON: I am sorry. You prefer silence.

CREON: Now, by God—!
I swear, by all the gods in heaven above us,
You'll watch it, I swear you shall!
    [to the SERVANTS]   Bring her out!
Bring the woman out! Let her die before his eyes!
Here, this instant, with her bridegroom beside her!

HAIMON: Not here, no; she will not die here, King.
And you will never see my face again.
Go on raving as long as you've a friend to endure you.
                                   [*Exit* HAIMON.]

CHORAGOS: Gone, gone.
Creon, a young man in a rage is dangerous!

CREON: Let him do, or dream to do, more than a man can.
He shall not save these girls from death.

CHORAGOS: These girls?
You have sentenced them both?

CREON: No, you are right.
  I will not kill the one whose hands are clean.

CHORAGOS: But Antigone?

CREON: I will carry her far away
  Out there in the wilderness, and lock her
  Living in a vault of stone. She shall have food,
  As the custom is, to absolve the State of her death.
  And there let her pray to the gods of hell:
  They are her only gods:
  Perhaps they will show her an escape from death,
  Or she may learn,
                         though late,
  That piety shown the dead is pity in vain.

                                        [*Exit* CREON.]

ODE III

CHORUS: Love, unconquerable
  Waster of rich men, keeper
  Of warm lights and all-night vigil
  In the soft face of a girl:
  Sea-wanderer, forest-visitor!
  Even the pure Immortals cannot escape you,
  And mortal man, in his one day's dusk,
  Trembles before your glory.

  Surely you swerve upon ruin
  The just man's consenting heart,
  As here you have made bright anger
  Strike between father and son—

And none has conquered but Love!
A girl's glance working the will of heaven:
Pleasure to her alone who mocks us,
Merciless Aphrodite.

SCENE IV

[ANTIGONE *enters, guarded.*]

CHORAGOS: But I can no longer stand in awe of this,
Nor, seeing what I see, keep back my tears.
Here is Antigone, passing to that chamber
Where all find sleep at last.

ANTIGONE: Look upon me, friends, and pity me
Turning back at the night's edge to say
Good-bye to the sun that shines for me no longer;
Now sleepy Death
Summons me down to Acheron, that cold shore:
There is no bridesong there, nor any music.

CHORUS: Yet not unpraised, not without a kind of honor,
You walk at last into the underworld;
Untouched by sickness, broken by no sword.
What woman has ever found your way to death?

ANTIGONE: How often I have heard the story of Niobe,
Tantalos' wretched daughter, how the stone
Clung fast about her, ivy-close: and they say
The rain falls endlessly
And sifting soft snow; her tears are never done.
I feel the loneliness of her death in mine.

CHORUS: But she was born of heaven, and you

Are woman, woman-born. If her death is yours,
A mortal woman's, is this not for you
Glory in our world and in the world beyond?

ANTIGONE: You laugh at me. Ah, friends, friends,
Can you not wait until I am dead? O Thebes,
O men many-charioted, in love with Fortune,
Dear springs of Dirce, sacred Theban grove,
Be witnesses for me, denied all pity,
Unjustly judged! and think a word of love
For her whose path turns
Under dark earth, where there are no more tears.

CHORUS: You have passed beyond human daring and come at last
Into a place of stone where Justice sits.
I cannot tell
What shape of your father's guilt appears in this.

ANTIGONE: You have touched it at last: that bridal bed
Unspeakable, horror of son and mother mingling:
Their crime, infection of all our family!
O Oedipus, father and brother!
Your marriage strikes from the grave to murder mine.
I have been a stranger here in my own land:
All my life
The blasphemy of my birth has followed me.

CHORUS: Reverence is a virtue, but strength
Lives in established law: that must prevail.
You have made your choice,
Your death is the doing of your conscious hand.

ANTIGONE: Then let me go, since all your words are bitter,

And the very light of the sun is cold to me.
Lead me to my vigil, where I must have
Neither love nor lamentation; no song, but silence.

CREON: If dirges and planned lamentations could put off
    death,
Men would be singing forever.
    [*to the* SERVANTS]   Take her, go!
You know your orders: take her to the vault
And leave her alone there. And if she lives or dies,
That's her affair, not ours: our hands are clean.

ANTIGONE: O tomb, vaulted bride-bed in eternal rock,
    Soon I shall be with my own again
    Where Persephone welcomes the thin ghosts
        underground:
    And I shall see my father again, and you, mother,
    And dearest Polyneices—
                            dearest indeed
    To me, since it was my hand
    That washed him clean and poured the ritual wine:
    And my reward is death before my time!

    And yet, as men's hearts know, I have done no wrong,
    I have not sinned before God. Or if I have,
    I shall know the truth in death. But if the guilt
    Lies upon Creon who judged me, then, I pray,
    May his punishment equal my own.

CHORAGOS: O passionate heart,
    Unyielding, tormented still by the same winds!

CREON: Her guards shall have good cause to regret their
    delaying.

ANTIGONE: Ah! That voice is like the voice of death!

CREON: I can give you no reason to think you are mistaken.

ANTIGONE: Thebes, and you my fathers' gods,
And rulers of Thebes, you see me now, the last
Unhappy daughter of a line of kings,
Your kings, led away to death. You will remember
What things I suffer, and at what men's hands,
Because I would not transgress the laws of heaven.
  [*to the* GUARDS]
Come: let us wait no longer.

[*Exit* ANTIGONE, *guarded.*]

ODE IV

CHORUS: All Danae's beauty was locked away
In a brazen cell where the sunlight could not come:
A small room, still as any grave, enclosed her.
Yet she was a princess too,
And Zeus in a rain of gold poured love upon her.
O child, child,
No power in wealth or war
Or tough sea-blackened ships
Can prevail against untiring Destiny!

And Dryas' son also, that furious king,
Bore the god's prisoning anger for his pride:
Sealed up by Dionysos in deaf stone,
His madness died among echoes.
So at the last he learned what dreadful power

His tongue had mocked:
For he had profaned the revels,
And fired the wrath of the nine
Implacable Sisters that love the sound of the flute.

And old men tell a half-remembered tale
Of horror done where a dark ledge splits the sea
And a double surf beats on the gray shores:
How a king's new woman, sick
With hatred for the queen he had imprisoned,
Ripped out his two sons' eyes with her bloody hands
While grinning Ares watched the shuttle plunge
Four times: four blind wounds crying for revenge,

Crying, tears and blood mingled.—Piteously born,
Those sons whose mother was of heavenly birth!
Her father was the god of the North Wind
And she was cradled by gales,
She raced with young colts on the glittering hills
And walked untrammeled in the open light:
But in her marriage deathless Fate found means
To build a tomb like yours for all her joy.

SCENE V

[Enter blind TEIRESIAS, *led by a boy.]*

TEIRESIAS: This is the way the blind man comes, Princes,
    Princes,
Lock-step, two heads lit by the eyes of one.

CREON: What new thing have you to tell us, old Teiresias?

TEIRESIAS: I have much to tell you: listen to the prophet, Creon.

CREON: I am not aware that I have ever failed to listen.

TEIRESIAS: Then you have done wisely, King, and ruled well.

CREON: I admit my debt to you. But what have you to say?

TEIRESIAS: This, Creon: you stand once more on the edge of fate.

CREON: What do you mean? Your words are a kind of dread.

TEIRESIAS: Listen, Creon:
I was sitting in my chair of augury, at the place
Where the birds gather about me. They were all
    a-chatter,
As is their habit, when suddenly I heard
A strange note in their jangling, a scream, a
Whirring fury; I knew that they were fighting,
Tearing each other, dying
In a whirlwind of wings clashing. And I was afraid.
I began the rites of burnt-offering at the altar,
But Hephaistos failed me: instead of bright flame,
There was only the sputtering slime of the fat thigh-flesh
Melting: the entrails dissolved in gray smoke,
The bare bone burst from the welter. And no blaze!

This was a sign from heaven. My boy described it,
Seeing for me as I see for others.

I tell you, Creon, you yourself have brought
This new calamity upon us. Our hearths and altars

Are stained with the corruption of dogs and carrion birds
That glut themselves on the corpse of Oedipus' son.
The gods are deaf when we pray to them, their fire
Recoils from our offering, their birds of omen
Have no cry of comfort, for they are gorged
With the thick blood of the dead.

        O my son,
These are no trifles! Think: all men make mistakes,
But a good man yields when he knows his course is
 wrong,
And repairs the evil. The only crime is pride.

Give in to the dead man, then: do not fight with a
 corpse—
What glory is it to kill a man who is dead?
Think, I beg you:
It is for your own good that I speak as I do.
You should be able to yield for your own good.

CREON: It seems that prophets have made me their
 especial province.
All my life long
I have been a kind of butt for the dull arrows
Of doddering fortune-tellers!

       No, Teiresias:
If your birds—if the great eagles of God himself
Should carry him stinking bit by bit to heaven,
I would not yield. I am not afraid of pollution:
No man can defile the gods.

       Do what you will,
Go into business, make money, speculate
In India gold or that synthetic gold from Sardis,
Get rich otherwise than by my consent to bury him.

Teiresias, it is a sorry thing when a wise man
Sells his wisdom, lets out his words for hire!

TEIRESIAS: Ah Creon! Is there no man left in the world—

CREON: To do what?—Come, let's have the aphorism!

TEIRESIAS: No man who knows that wisdom outweighs any
wealth?

CREON: As surely as bribes are baser than any baseness.

TEIRESIAS: You are sick, Creon! You are deathly sick!

CREON: As you say: it is not my place to challenge a
prophet.

TEIRESIAS: Yet you have said my prophecy is for sale.

CREON: The generation of prophets has always loved gold.

TEIRESIAS: The generation of kings has always loved brass.

CREON: You forget yourself! You are speaking to your
King.

TEIRESIAS: I know it. You are a king because of me.

CREON: You have a certain skill; but you have sold out.

TEIRESIAS: King, you will drive me to words that—

CREON: Say them, say them!
Only remember: I will not pay you for them.

TEIRESIAS: No, you will find them too costly.

CREON: No doubt. Speak:
Whatever you say, you will not change my will.

TEIRESIAS: Then take this, and take it to heart!

The time is not far off when you shall pay back
Corpse for corpse, flesh of your own flesh.
You have thrust the child of this world into living night,
You have kept from the gods below the child that is
    theirs:
The one in a grave before her death, the other,
Dead, denied the grave. This is your crime:
And the Furies and the dark gods of Hell
Are swift with terrible punishment for you.

Do you want to buy me now, Creon?

                        Not many days,
And your house will be full of men and women weeping,
And curses will be hurled at you from far
Cities grieving for sons unburied, left to rot
Before the walls of Thebes.

These are my arrows, Creon: they are all for you.
   [*to* BOY]
But come, child: lead me home.
Let him waste his fine anger upon younger men.
Maybe he will learn at last
To control a wiser tongue in a better head.

                        [*Exit* TEIRESIAS.]

CHORAGOS: The old man has gone, King, but his words
  Remain to plague us. I am old, too,
  But I cannot remember that he was ever false.

CREON: That is true.... It troubles me.
  Oh it is hard to give in! but it is worse
  To risk everything for stubborn pride.

CHORAGOS: Creon: take my advice.

CREON: What shall I do?

CHORAGOS: Go quickly: free Antigone from her vault
  And build a tomb for the body of Polyneices.

CREON: You would have me do this?

CHORAGOS: Creon, yes!
  And it must be done at once: God moves
  Swiftly to cancel the folly of stubborn men.

CREON: It is hard to deny the heart! But I
  Will do it: I will not fight with destiny.

CHORAGOS: You must go yourself, you cannot leave it to
  others.

CREON: I will go.
               —Bring axes, servants:
  Come with me to the tomb. I buried her, I
  Will set her free.
               Oh quickly!
  My mind misgives—
  The laws of the gods are mighty, and a man must serve
    them
  To the last day of his life!

[*Exit* CREON.]

PAEAN

CHORAGOS: God of many names

CHORUS: O Iacchos

                                          son
of Cadmeian Semele
                    O born of the Thunder!
Guardian of the West
                        Regent
of Eleusis' plain
                    O Prince of maenad Thebes
and the Dragon Field by rippling Ismenos:

CHORAGOS: God of many names

CHORUS: the flame of torches
flares on our hills
                    the nymphs of Iacchos
dance at the spring of Castalia:

from the vine-close mountain
                                come ah come in ivy:
Evohe evohe! sings through the streets of Thebes

CHORAGOS: God of many names

CHORUS: Iacchos of Thebes
heavenly Child
                    of Semele bride of the Thunderer!
The shadow of plague is upon us:
                                come
with clement feet
                    oh come from Parnasos
down the long slopes
                        across the lamenting water

CHORAGOS: Io Fire! Chorister of the throbbing stars!

O purest among the voices of the night!
Thou son of God, blaze for us!

CHORUS: Come with choric rapture of circling Maenads
Who cry to *Io Iacche!*
                    God of many names!

EXODOS

                                    [*Enter* MESSENGER.]

MESSENGER: Men of the line of Cadmos, you who live
Near Amphion's citadel:
                    I cannot say
Of any condition of human life "This is fixed,
This is clearly good, or bad." Fate raises up,
And Fate casts down the happy and unhappy alike:
No man can foretell his Fate.
                              Take the case of Creon:
Creon was happy once, as I count happiness:
Victorious in battle, sole governor of the land,
Fortunate father of children nobly born.
And now it has all gone from him! Who can say
That a man is still alive when his life's joy fails?
He is a walking dead man. Grant him rich,
Let him live like a king in his great house:
If his pleasure is gone, I would not give
So much as the shadow of smoke for all he owns.

CHORAGOS: Your words hint at sorrow: what is your news for
us?

MESSENGER: They are dead. The living are guilty of their
death.

CHORAGOS: Who is guilty? Who is dead? Speak!

MESSENGER: Haimon.
Haimon is dead; and the hand that killed him
Is his own hand.

CHORAGOS: His father's? or his own?

MESSENGER: His own, driven mad by the murder his father
had done.

CHORAGOS: Teiresias, Teiresias, how clearly you saw it all!

MESSENGER: This is my news: you must draw what
conclusions you can from it.

CHORAGOS: But look: Eurydice, our Queen:
Has she overheard us?

> [*Enter* EURYDICE *from the Palace.*]

EURYDICE: I have heard something, friends:
As I was unlocking the gate of Pallas' shrine,
For I needed her help today, I heard a voice
Telling of some new sorrow. And I fainted
There at the temple with all my maidens about me.
But speak again: whatever it is, I can bear it:
Grief and I are no strangers.

MESSENGER: Dearest Lady,
I will tell you plainly all that I have seen.
I shall not try to comfort you: what is the use,
Since comfort could lie only in what is not true?
The truth is always best.
                          I went with Creon
To the outer plain where Polyneices was lying,
No friend to pity him, his body shredded by dogs.
We made our prayers in that place to Hecate

And Pluto, that they would be merciful. And we bathed
The corpse with holy water, and we brought
Fresh-broken branches to burn what was left of it,
And upon the urn we heaped up a towering barrow
Of the earth of his own land.

                     When we were done, we ran
To the vault where Antigone lay on her couch of stone.
One of the servants had gone ahead,
And while he was yet far off he heard a voice
Grieving within the chamber, and he came back
And told Creon. And as the King went closer,
The air was full of wailing, the words lost,
And he begged us to make all haste. "Am I a prophet?"
He said, weeping, "And must I walk this road,
The saddest of all that I have gone before?
My son's voice calls on me. Oh quickly, quickly!
Look through the crevice there, and tell me
If it is Haimon, or some deception of the gods!"

We obeyed; and in the cavern's farthest corner
We saw her lying:
She had made a noose of her fine linen veil
And hanged herself. Haimon lay beside her,
His arms about her waist, lamenting her,
His love lost under ground, crying out
That his father had stolen her away from him.

When Creon saw him the tears rushed to his eyes
And he called to him: "What have you done, child?
   Speak to me.
What are you thinking that makes your eyes so strange?
O my son, my son, I come to you on my knees!"
But Haimon spat in his face. He said not a word,

Staring—
         And suddenly drew his sword
And lunged. Creon shrank back, the blade missed; and
   the boy,
Desperate against himself, drove it half its length
Into his own side, and fell. And as he died
He gathered Antigone close in his arms again,
Choking, his blood bright red on her white cheek.
And now he lies dead with the dead, and she is his
At last, his bride in the houses of the dead.

                              [*Exit* EURYDICE *into the Palace.*]

CHORAGOS: She has left us without a word. What can this
mean?

MESSENGER: It troubles me, too; yet she knows what is
   best,
Her grief is too great for public lamentation,
And doubtless she has gone to her chamber to weep
For her dead son, leading her maidens in his dirge.

CHORAGOS: It may be so: but I fear this deep silence.

MESSENGER: I will see what she is doing. I will go in.

                         [*Exit* MESSENGER *into the Palace.*]

         [*Enter* CREON *with attendants, bearing* HAIMON'S *body.*]

CHORAGOS: But here is the King himself: oh look at him,
Bearing his own damnation in his arms.

CREON: Nothing you say can touch me any more.
My own blind heart has brought me
From darkness to final darkness. Here you see
The father murdering, the murdered son—
And all my civic wisdom!

Haimon my son, so young, so young to die,
I was the fool, not you; and you died for me.

CHORAGOS: That is the truth; but you were late in learning
it.

CREON: This truth is hard to bear. Surely a god
Has crushed me beneath the hugest weight of heaven,
And driven me headlong a barbaric way
To trample out the thing I held most dear.

The pains that men will take to come to pain!

[*Enter* MESSENGER *from the Palace.*]

MESSENGER: The burden you carry in your hands is
heavy,
But it is not all: you will find more in your house.

CREON: What burden worse than this shall I find there?

MESSENGER: The Queen is dead.

CREON: O port of death, deaf world,
Is there no pity for me? And you, Angel of evil,
I was dead, and your words are death again.
Is it true, boy? Can it be true?
Is my wife dead? Has death bred death?

MESSENGER: You can see for yourself.

[*The doors are opened, and
the body of* EURYDICE *is disclosed within.*]

CREON: Oh pity!
All true, all true, and more than I can bear!
O my wife, my son!

MESSENGER: She stood before the altar, and her heart
Welcomed the knife her own hand guided,
And a great cry burst from her lips for Megareus dead,
And for Haimon dead, her sons; and her last breath
Was a curse for their father, the murderer of her sons.
And she fell, and the dark flowed in through her closing
eyes

CREON: O God, I am sick with fear.
Are there no swords here? Has no one a blow for me?

MESSENGER: Her curse is upon you for the deaths of both.

CREON: It is right that it should be. I alone am guilty.
I know it, and I say it. Lead me in,
Quickly, friends.
I have neither life nor substance. Lead me in.

CHORAGOS: You are right, if there can be right in so
much wrong.
The briefest way is best in a world of sorrow.

CREON: Let it come,
Let death come quickly, and be kind to me.
I would not ever see the sun again.

CHORAGOS: All that will come when it will; but we,
meanwhile,
Have much to do. Leave the future to itself.

CREON: All my heart was in that prayer!

CHORAGOS: Then do not pray any more: the sky is deaf.

CREON: Lead me away. I have been rash and foolish.
I have killed my son and my wife.
I look for comfort; my comfort lies here dead.

Whatever my hands have touched has come to nothing.
Fate has brought all my pride to a thought of dust.

[*As* CREON *is being led into the house,*
the CHORAGOS *advances and speaks directly to the audience.*]

CHORAGOS: There is no happiness where there is no
   wisdom;
No wisdom but in submission to the gods.
Big words are always punished,
And proud men in old age learn to be wise.

Interpretive Questions

1. Why does the Chorus think Antigone is wrong
   throughout most of the play?

2. Is Antigone doomed because she is the daughter of
   Oedipus, or does she make her own fate?

3. Why does Creon reverse the order of actions the
   Chroragus recommends, and bury Polyneices before he
   frees Antigone?

4. Does Creon refuse to change his edict because he is sure
   he is right or because he is afraid to admit he is wrong?

5. Why does the Chorus find merit in what both Haimon
   and his father say to each other in their argument?

PRACTICE

Writing Interpretive Questions
"Antigone"

A reader made notes on a passage from *Antigone*
and then developed some of them into
interpretive questions.

tempting fate:
challenging
Creon?

CHORUS: You have passed beyond
                human daring and come at last

cave [Into a place of stone where <u>Justice</u> sits.
        I cannot tell   whose?

Chorus
not sure [What shape of your father's guilt
            appears in this.

Antigone
relieved? [ANTIGONE: You have touched it at
                last: that bridal bed

Antigone
blames parents

        Unspeakable, horror of son and
            mother mingling:
        Their crime, infection of all our family!
        O Oedipus, father and brother!

Only mention
of her marriage [Your marriage strikes from the grave
                    to murder mine.

why? [I have been a stranger here in my
        own land:
    All my life
    The blasphemy of my birth has
        followed me.

1. Is the Chorus accusing Antigone of tempting fate or of challenging Creon?

2. Whose justice does Antigone face in the cave: Creon's or the gods'?

3. Is Antigone relieved when the Chorus suggests she is not wholly responsible for her actions?

4. Does Antigone think that her parents' sin is the cause of her misfortune?

5. Why does Antigone speak of her own marriage only once in the play, and then describe it as the victim of her parents' marriage?

Using the example you have just read as a guide, make your own notes on the following passage, then turn those notes into interpretive questions.

CHORUS: Reverence is a virtue, but strength
Lives in established law: that must prevail.
You have made your choice,
Your death is the doing of your conscious hand.

ANTIGONE: Then let me go, since all your
      words are bitter,
And the very light of the sun is cold to me.
Lead me to my vigil, where I must have
Neither love nor lamentation; no song,
      but silence.

_____

_____

_____

_____

X

By and About Alexis de Tocqueville

(1804–1859)

From May 1831 to February 1832, Alexis de Tocqueville observed democratic politics and society as he traveled in the United States. *Democracy in America,* the record of his observations, brought Tocqueville international recognition.

After a month of travel, Tocqueville wrote to his father about the relative value of political institutions:

> The more I see this country the more I admit myself penetrated with this truth: that there is nothing absolute in the theoretical value of political institutions, and that their efficiency depends almost always on the original circumstances and the social condition of the people to whom they are applied. I see institutions succeed here which would infallibly turn France upside down; others which suit us would obviously do harm in America; and yet, either I am much mistaken, or man is neither other nor better here than with us. Only he is otherwise placed.

In *Democracy in America,* he commented on self-interest in relation to morality:

> The principle of self-interest rightly understood produces no great acts of self-sacrifice, but it suggests daily small acts of self-denial. By itself it cannot suffice to make a man virtuous; but it disciplines a number of persons in habits of regularity, temperance, moderation, foresight, self-command; and if it does not lead men straight to virtue by the will, it gradually draws them in that direction by their habits.... The principle of interest rightly understood perhaps prevents men from rising far above the level of mankind, but a great number of other men, who were falling far below it, are caught and restrained by it. Observe some few individuals, they are lowered by it; survey mankind, they are raised.

On majority rule:

> A majority taken collectively is only an individual whose opinions, and frequently whose interests, are opposed to those of another individual who is styled a minority. If it be admitted that a man

possessing absolute power may misuse that power by wronging his adversaries, why should not a majority be liable to the same reproach?

On reelecting the president:

It is impossible to consider the ordinary course of affairs in the United States without perceiving that the desire to be re-elected is the chief aim of the President; that the whole policy of his administration, and even his most indifferent measures, tend to this object; and that, especially as the crisis approaches, his personal interest takes the place of his interest in the public good. The principle of re-eligibility renders the corrupting influence of elective government still more extensive and pernicious.

Early in the nineteenth century the European aristocracy had much to fear from democracy, for it threatened to destroy the stable, orderly, and customary society in which the aristocracy held special privileges and authority. Moreover, it threatened to do so by means of violent revolution. Alexis de Tocqueville, a French aristocrat, believed that the push for democracy was irresistible and that the aristocrats would have to come to terms with it. He wrote Democracy in America *to give them the information they needed to understand democracy and to find their place in it. In our selection, Tocqueville addresses the fear that the equality of social conditions may encourage revolution. He argues that, on the contrary, equality leads people to resist substantial changes in the way of life—and that this can be a danger in itself.*

Why Great Revolutions Will Become Rare

Alexis de Tocqueville

When a people has lived for centuries under a system of castes and classes, it can only reach a democratic state of society through a long series of more or less painful transformations. These must involve violent efforts and many vicissitudes, in the course of which property, opinions, and power are all subject to swift changes.

Even when this great revolution has come to an end, the revolutionary habits created thereby and by the profound disturbances thereon ensuing will long endure.

As all this takes place just at the time when social conditions are being leveled, the conclusion has been drawn that there must be a hidden connection and secret link between equality itself and revolutions, so that neither can occur without the other.

On this point reason and experience seem agreed.

Among a people where ranks are more or less equal, there

---

*A selection from *Democracy in America*.

193

is no apparent connection between men to hold them firmly in place. None of them has any permanent right or power to give commands, and none is bound by his social condition to obey. Each man, having some education and some resources, can choose his own road and go along separately from all the rest.

The same causes which make the citizens independent of each other daily prompt new and restless longings and constantly goad them on.

It therefore seems natural to suppose that in a democratic society ideas, things, and men must eternally be changing shape and position and that ages of democracy must be times of swift and constant transformation.

But is this in fact so? Does equality of social conditions habitually and permanently drive men toward revolutions? Does it contain some disturbing principle which prevents society from settling down and inclines the citizens constantly to change their laws, principles, and mores? I do not think so. The subject is important, and I ask the reader to follow my argument closely.

Almost every revolution which has changed the shape of nations has been made to consolidate or destroy inequality. Disregarding the secondary causes which have had some effect on the great convulsions in the world, you will almost always find that equality was at the heart of the matter. Either the poor were bent on snatching the property of the rich, or the rich were trying to hold the poor down. So, then, if you could establish a state of society in which each man had something to keep and little to snatch, you would have done much for the peace of the world.

I realize that among a great people there will always be some very poor and some very rich citizens. But the poor, instead of forming the vast majority of the population as is always the case in aristocratic societies, are but few, and the law has not drawn them together by the link of an irremediable and hereditary state of wretchedness.

The rich, on their side, are scattered and powerless. They have no conspicuous privileges, and even their wealth, being no longer incorporated and bound up with the soil, is impalpable and, as it were, invisible. As there is no longer a race of poor men, so there is not a race of rich men; the rich daily rise out of the crowd and constantly return thither. Hence they do not form a distinct class, easily identified and plundered; moreover, there are a thousand hidden threads connecting them with the mass of citizens, so that the people would hardly know how to attack them without harming itself. In democratic societies between these two extremes there is an innumerable crowd who are much alike, who, though not exactly rich nor yet quite poor, have enough property to want order and not enough to excite envy.

Such men are the natural enemies of violent commotion; their immobility keeps all above and below them quiet, and assures the stability of the body social.

I am not suggesting that they are themselves satisfied with their actual position or that they would feel any natural abhorrence toward a revolution if they could share the plunder without suffering the calamities; on the contrary, their eagerness to get rich is unparalleled, but their trouble is to know whom to despoil. The same social condition which prompts their longings restrains them within necessary limits. It gives men both greater freedom to change and less interest in doing so.

Not only do men in democracies feel no natural inclination for revolutions, but they are afraid of them.

Any revolution is more or less a threat to property. Most inhabitants of a democracy have property. And not only have they got property, but they live in the conditions in which men attach most value to property.

If one studies each class of which society is composed closely, it is easy to see that passions due to ownership are keenest among the middle classes.

The poor often do not trouble much about their possessions, for their suffering from what they lack is much greater than their enjoyment of what they have. The rich have many other passions to gratify besides those connected with wealth, and moreover, the long and troublesome management of a great fortune sometimes makes them in the end insensible to its charms.

But men whose comfortable existence is equally far from wealth and poverty set immense value on their possessions. As they are still very close to poverty, they see its privations in detail and are afraid of them; nothing but a scanty fortune, the cynosure of all their hopes and fears, keeps them therefrom. The constant care which it occasions daily attaches them to their property; their continual exertions to increase it make it even more precious to them. The idea of giving up the smallest part of it is insufferable to them, and the thought of losing it completely strikes them as the worst of all evils. Now, it is just the number of the eager and restless small property-owners which equality of conditions constantly increases.

Hence the majority of citizens in a democracy do not see clearly what they could gain by a revolution, but they constantly see a thousand ways in which they could lose by one.

I have shown elsewhere in this work how equality naturally leads men to go in for industry and trade and that it tends to increase and distribute real property. I pointed out that it inspires every man with a constant and eager desire to increase his well-being. Nothing is more opposed to revolutionary passions than all this.

The final result of a revolution might serve the interests of industry and trade, but its first effect will almost always be the ruin of industrialists and traders, because it must always immediately change general habits of consumption and temporarily upset the balance between supply and demand.

Moreover, I know nothing more opposed to revolutionary morality than the moral standards of traders. Trade is the natural enemy of all violent passions. Trade loves moderation, delights in compromise, and is most careful to avoid anger. It is patient, supple, and insinuating, only resorting to extreme measures in cases of absolute necessity. Trade makes men independent of one another and gives them a high idea of their personal importance; it leads them to want to manage their own affairs and teaches them how to succeed therein. Hence it makes them inclined to liberty but disinclined to revolution.

In a revolution the owners of personal property have more to fear than all others, for their property is often both easy to seize and capable of disappearing completely at any moment. Owners of land have less to fear on this score, for although they may lose the income therefrom, they can hope at least to keep the land itself through the greatest vicissitudes. For this reason one finds that the latter are much less frightened of revolutionary movements than the former.

Therefore the more widely personal property is distributed and increased and the greater the number of those enjoying it, the less is a nation inclined to revolution.

Moreover, whatever a man's calling and whatever type of property he owns, one characteristic is common to all.

No one is fully satisfied with his present fortune, and all are constantly trying a thousand various ways to improve it. Consider any individual at any period of his life, and you will always find him preoccupied with fresh plans to increase his comfort. Do not talk to him about the interests and rights of the human race; that little private business of his for the moment absorbs all his thoughts, and he hopes that public disturbances can be put off to some other time.

This not only prevents them from causing revolutions but also deters them from wanting them. Violent political passions have little hold on men whose whole thoughts are bent on the pursuit of well-being. Their excitement about small matters makes them calm about great ones.

It is true that from time to time in democratic societies aspiring and ambitious citizens do arise who are not content to follow the beaten track. Such men love revolutions and hail their approach. But they have great difficulty in bringing them about unless extraordinary events play into their hands.

No man can struggle with advantage against the spirit of his age and country, and however powerful a man may be, it is hard for him to make his contemporaries share feelings and ideas which run counter to the general run of their hopes and desires. It is therefore a mistake to suppose that once equality has become something long-established and undisputed, molding manners to its taste, men will easily allow themselves to be thrown into danger by some rash leader or bold innovator.

I am not suggesting that they resist him openly by means of well-thought-out schemes, or indeed by means of any considered determination to resist. They show no energy in fighting him and sometimes even applaud him, but they do not follow him. Secretly their apathy is opposed to his fire, their conservative interests to his revolutionary instincts, their homely tastes to his adventurous passion, their common sense to his flighty genius, their prose to his poetry. With immense effort he rouses them for a moment, but they soon slip from him and fall back, as it were, by their own weight. He exhausts himself trying to animate this indifferent and preoccupied crowd and finds at last that he is reduced to impotence, not because he is conquered but because he is alone.

I am not making out that the inhabitants of democracies are by nature stationary; on the contrary, I think that such a society is always on the move and that no member thereof knows what rest is; but I think that all bestir themselves within certain limits which they hardly ever pass. Daily they change, alter, and renew things of secondary importance, but they are very careful not to touch fundamentals. They love change, but they are afraid of revolutions.

Although the Americans are constantly modifying or repealing some of their laws, they are far from showing any revolutionary passions. One can easily see, by the promptness with which they stop and calm themselves just when public agitation begins to be threatening and when passions seem most excited, that they fear a revolution as the greatest of evils and that each of them is inwardly resolved to make great sacrifices to avoid one. In no other country in the world is the love of property keener or more alert than in the United States, and nowhere else does the majority display less inclination toward doctrines which in any way threaten the way property is owned.

I have often noted that theories which are basically revolutionary in that they cannot be put into practice without a complete, in some cases a sudden, change in property rights and personal status are infinitely less in favor in the United States than in the great monarchies of Europe. Though some individuals profess them, the mass of the people reject them with instinctive horror.

I have no hesitation in saying that most of the maxims which are generally called democratic in France would be outlawed by the American democracy. That is easily understood. In America there exist democratic ideas and passions; in Europe we still have revolutionary ones.

If there ever are great revolutions there, they will be caused by the presence of the blacks upon American soil. That is to say, it will not be the equality of social conditions but rather their inequality which may give rise thereto.

When social conditions are equal, every man tends to live apart, centered in himself and forgetful of the public. Should democratic legislators not seek to correct this fatal tendency, or actually favor it, thinking that it diverts the citizens' attention from political passions and avoids revolutions, it might happen in the end that they may bring about that very evil which they seek to avoid and that the moment may come when the unruly passions of certain men, aided by the foolish selfishness and pusillanimity of the greater number, will in the end subject the fabric of society to strange vicissitudes.

In democratic societies it is only small minorities who desire revolutions, but the minorities may bring them about.

I am far from asserting that democratic nations are safe from revolutions; I only say that the social state of those nations does not lead toward revolution, but rather wards it off. Democratic nations, left to themselves, are slow to embark on great adventures; they are only dragged into revolutions in spite of themselves; they may sometimes suffer from them, but they never make them. I would add that once they have gained education and experience, they will not allow them to occur.

I am well aware that, in this context, public institutions may have great influence; they can favor or restrain the instincts bred by the social state. I must therefore again make it perfectly clear that a nation is not safe from revolution simply because social conditions are equal there. But I do think that, whatever institutions such a people may have, great revolutions will be infinitely less violent and rarer than is generally supposed. I can easily, though vaguely, foresee a political condition, combined with equality, which might create a society more stationary than any we have ever known in our Western world.

What I have been saying about facts applies, in part, to ideas.

Two things in America are astonishing: the changeableness of most human behavior and the strange stability of certain principles. Men are constantly on the move, but the spirit of humanity seems almost unmoved.

Once an opinion has spread on American soil and taken root there, it would seem that no power on earth can eradicate it. In the United States general doctrines concerning religion, philosophy, morality, and even politics do not vary at all, or at least are only modified by the slow and often unconscious working of some hidden process. Even the very crudest prejudices take an unconscionable time to efface, in spite of all the froth and stir of men and things.

One hears people say that it is inherent in the habits and nature of democracies to change feelings and thoughts at every moment. That may have been true of such small democratic nations as those of antiquity, where everyone could assemble in the marketplace, and when there, be carried away by an orator's eloquence. But I have never seen anything like that happening in the great democracy on the other side of our ocean. What struck me most in the United States was the difficulty experienced in getting an idea, once conceived, out of the head of the majority and stopping their following the man of their choice. Neither writings nor speeches can have much success in that; only experience can do it, and that too must sometimes be repeated.

That is surprising at first sight, but closer examination gives the explanation.

I do not think it as easy as is generally supposed to eradicate the prejudices of a democratic people, to change its beliefs, to substitute new religious, philosophical, political, and moral principles for those which have once become established, in a word, to bring about great or frequent mental revolutions.

Not that there the human mind is lazy; it is constantly active, but it is more concerned with infinite variations in the consequences to be derived from known principles and in finding new consequences rather than in seeking new principles. It turns around spryly on itself but has no straightforward impulse to rapid progress; slight, continual, hasty movements gradually extend its orbit, but it never changes position all at once.

Men with equal rights, education, and wealth, that is to say, men who are in just the same condition, must have very similar needs, habits, and tastes. As they see things in the same light, their minds naturally incline to similar ideas, and though any one of them could part company with the rest and work out his own beliefs, in the end they all concur, unconsciously and unintentionally, in a certain number of common opinions.

The more closely I consider the effects of equality upon the mind, the more I am convinced that the intellectual anarchy which we see around us is not, as some suppose, the natural state for democracies. I think we should rather consider it as an accidental characteristic peculiar to their youth, and something that only happens during that transitional period when men have broken the ancient links which held them together, but are still immensely different in origin, education, and manners. In such circumstances, having preserved very various ideas, instincts, and tastes, nothing any longer prevents them from airing them. Men's main opinions become alike as the conditions of their lives become alike. That seems to be the general and permanent fact; the rest is fortuitous and ephemeral.

It must, I think, be rare in a democracy for a man suddenly to conceive a system of ideas far different from those accepted by his contemporaries; and I suppose that, even should such an innovator arise, he would have great difficulty in making himself heard to begin with, and even more in convincing people.

When conditions are almost equal, one man is not easily to be persuaded by another. When all men see each other at close quarters, have together learned the same things and led the same life, there is no natural inclination for them to accept one of their number as a guide and follow him blindly; one hardly ever takes on trust the opinion of an equal of like standing with oneself.

It is not simply that in democracies confidence in the superior knowledge of certain individuals has been weakened. As I have pointed out before, the general idea that any man whosoever can attain an intellectual superiority beyond the reach of the rest is soon cast in doubt.

As men grow more like each other, a dogma concerning intellectual equality gradually creeps into their beliefs, and it becomes harder for any innovator whosoever to gain and maintain great influence over the mind of a nation. In such societies sudden intellectual revolutions must therefore be rare. For, taking a general view of world history, one finds that it is less the force of an argument than the authority of a name which has brought about great and rapid changes in accepted ideas.

It is also important to realize that since there is no link binding the inhabitants of democracies to each other, each man has to be convinced separately, whereas in aristocracies it is enough to influence the views of certain individuals, and the rest will follow. If Luther had lived in an age of equality and there had been no great territorial magnates and princes to listen to him, perhaps he would have found it harder to change the face of Europe.

Not that the inhabitants of democracies are naturally strongly convinced of the certainty of their beliefs; they often feel doubts which, in their view, no one can resolve. It sometimes happens in such times that a change of intellectual position is desired, but without the strong pressure of any directing force, nothing more than oscillation to and fro, without any progress, occurs.*

Even when one has won the confidence of a democratic nation, it is a hard matter to attract its attention. It is very difficult to make the inhabitants of democracies listen when one is not talking about themselves. They do not hear what is said to them because they are always very preoccupied with what they are doing.

Indeed, there are few men of leisure in democracies. Life passes in movement and noise, and men are so busy acting that they have little time to think. I want especially to stress that they are not only busy, but passionately interested in their business. They are always in action, and each action absorbs all their faculties. The fire they put into their work prevents their being fired by ideas.

---

* Trying to discover the state of society most favorable to great intellectual revolutions, I think it must lie somewhere between complete equality for every citizen and the absolute separation of classes.

Under a caste system generation follows generation without a change in man's position; while some have nothing more to desire, the rest have nothing better to hope. The imagination slumbers in the stillness of this universal silence, and the mere idea of movement does not come into men's minds.

When classes have been abolished and conditions have become almost equal, men are constantly on the move, but each individual is isolated, on his own, and weak. For all the vast difference between these two states, they are alike in one respect, namely, that great intellectual revolutions become rare.

But between these two extremes in a nation's history there is an intermediate stage, a glorious yet troubled time in which conditions are not sufficiently fixed for the mind to sleep and in which there is enough inequality for men to exercise great power over the minds of others, so that a few can modify the beliefs of all. That is the time when great reformers arise and new ideas change the face of the world (*author's note*).

I think it is an arduous undertaking to excite the enthusiasm of a democratic nation for any theory which does not have a visible, direct, and immediate bearing on the occupations of their daily lives. Such a people does not easily give up its ancient beliefs. For it is enthusiasm which makes men's minds leap off the beaten track and brings about great intellectual, as well as political, revolutions.

Hence democratic nations have neither leisure nor taste to think out new opinions. Even when they are doubtful about accepted ideas they still stick to them because it would take too much time to examine and change them. They hold to them not because they are certain but because they are accepted.

There are also other, and even stronger, reasons which prevent any great change in the doctrines of a democratic people coming about easily. I have already indicated them at the beginning of this book.

Whereas, in such a nation, the influence of individuals is weak and almost nonexistent, the power of the mass over each individual mind is very great. I have given the reasons elsewhere. What I want to stress now is that it would be a mistake to suppose that this depends on nothing but the form of government and that the majority would lose its intellectual sway with its political power.

In aristocracies men often have something of greatness and strength which is all their own. When they find themselves at variance with most of their fellows, they retreat into themselves and there find support and consolation. But in democracies it is not like that. There public favor seems as necessary as the air they breathe, and to be out of harmony with the mass is, if one may put it so, no life at all. The mass has no need of laws to bend those who do not agree to its will. Its disapproval is enough. The sense of their isolation and impotence at once overwhelms them and drives them to despair.

Whenever conditions are equal, public opinion brings immense weight to bear on every individual. It surrounds, directs, and oppresses him. The basic constitution of society has more to do with this than any political laws. The more alike men are, the weaker each feels in the face of all. Finding nothing that raises him above their level and distinguishes him, he loses his self-confidence when he comes into collision with them. Not only does he mistrust his own strength, but even comes to doubt his own judgment, and he is brought very near to recognizing that he must be wrong when the majority hold the opposite view. There is no need for the majority to compel him; it convinces him.

Therefore, however powers within a democracy are organized and weighted, it will always be very difficult for a man to believe what the mass rejects and to profess what it condemns.

This circumstance is wonderfully favorable to the stability of beliefs.

When an opinion has taken root in a democracy and established itself in the minds of the majority, it afterward persists by itself, needing no effort to maintain it since no one attacks it. Those who at first rejected it as false come in the end to adopt it as accepted, and even those who still at the bottom of their hearts oppose it keep their views to themselves, taking great care to avoid a dangerous and futile contest.

It is true that when a democratic majority does change its mind, a sudden, arbitrary, and strange intellectual revolution may ensue. But yet that majority's opinion has great difficulty in changing, and it is almost as difficult to be sure that it has changed.

Sometimes, though no change may be visible from outside, it does happen that time, circumstances, and the lonely workings of each man's thought do, little by little, in the end shake or destroy some belief. It has not been openly attacked. No meetings have been held to fight against it. But one by one its supporters quietly drop it, so that finally these small continual defections leave it with but a few upholders.

In such conditions it still prevails.

As its opponents still hold their peace or only stealthily exchange their thoughts, they are themselves long unsure that a great revolution has taken place, and when in doubt, they take no action. They watch and keep quiet. The majority no longer believes, but it looks as if it did believe, and this empty ghost of public opinion is enough to chill the innovators and make them maintain their silent respect.

We live in a time that has witnessed the swiftest changes in men's minds. But yet perhaps some of the main opinions of mankind may be soon more stable than ever before in the centuries of our history. Such a time has not yet come, but it may be at hand.

The more closely I examine the needs and instincts natural to democracies, the more am I convinced that if ever equality is established generally and permanently in the world, great intellectual and political revolutions will become much more difficult and much rarer than is generally supposed.

Because the inhabitants of democracies always seem excited, uncertain, hurried, and ready to change both their minds and their situation, it has been supposed that they want immediately to abolish their laws, adopt new beliefs, and conform to new manners. It has not been noted that while equality leads men to make changes it also prompts them to have interests which require stability for their satisfaction; it both drives them on and holds them back; it goads them on and keeps their feet on the ground; it kindles their desires and limits their powers.

That is something which one does not see at first sight. The passions that keep the inhabitants of democracies separated from each other are obvious enough, but the hidden force which holds them back and holds them together is not obvious at a glance.

Can I safely say this amid the surrounding ruins? What I most fear for succeeding generations is not revolutions.

If the citizens continue to shut themselves up more and more narrowly in the little circle of petty domestic interests and keep themselves constantly busy therein, there is a danger that they may in the end become practically out of reach of those great and powerful public emotions which do indeed perturb peoples but which also make them grow and refresh them. Seeing property change hands so quickly, and love of property become so anxious and eager, I cannot help fearing that men may reach a point where they look on every new theory as a danger, every innovation as a toilsome trouble, every social advance as a first step toward revolution, and that they may absolutely refuse to move at all for fear of being carried off their feet. The prospect really does frighten me that they may finally become so engrossed in a cowardly love of immediate pleasures that their interest in their own future and in that of their descendants may vanish, and that they will prefer tamely to follow the course of their destiny rather than make a sudden energetic effort necessary to set things right.

People suppose that the new societies are going to change shape daily, but my fear is that they will end up by being too unalterably fixed with the same institutions, prejudices, and mores, so that mankind will stop progressing and will dig itself in. I fear that the mind may keep folding itself up in a narrower compass forever without producing new ideas, that men will wear themselves out in trivial, lonely, futile activity, and that for all its constant agitation humanity will make no advance.

Interpretive Questions

1. Why does equality lead to a greater stress on materialistic values?

2. Does a society that never has a political or intellectual revolution run the risk of stagnating?

3. Does Tocqueville believe that both political and intellectual revolutions are based on material interests? Does he think people would revolt for nonmaterialistic reasons, such as freedom of speech, freedom of the press, and freedom of religion?

4. Why does Tocqueville anticipate that equality may lead to a leveling down of intellectual life rather than to a raising of standards?

5. Is political revolution desirable under some circumstances in a democratic society, according to Tocqueville?

XI

By and About Virginia Woolf

(1882—1941)

Virginia Woolf was one of England's foremost novelists and critics during the fertile years of artistic experimentation and discovery between the two world wars. A friend and fellow artist once remarked that she "liked writing with an intensity which few writers have attained, or even desired." She was an equally passionate and gifted reader, and in "How Should One Read A Book" she discusses the complexity of the reading process.

As Woolf sees it, reading is a two-part process, the first step being "to receive impressions with the utmost understanding, the second to pass judgment." Woolf does not pretend that the second part of reading, making comparisons and judgments, is as simple as the first:

> To continue reading without the book before you, to hold one shadow-shape against another, to have read widely enough and with enough understanding to make such comparisons alive and illuminating—that is difficult; it is still more difficult to press further and to say, "Not only is the book of this sort, but it is of this value; here it fails; here it succeeds; this is bad; that is good." To carry out this part of a reader's duty needs such imagination, insight, and learning that it is hard to conceive any one mind sufficiently endowed; impossible for the most self-confident to find more than the seeds of such powers in himself.

Would it not be wiser then, she asks, to leave this difficult business to the critics? Her answer is no, we must judge for ourselves:

> And even if the results are abhorrent and our judgments are wrong, still our taste, the nerve of sensation that sends shocks through us, is our chief illuminant; we learn through feeling; we cannot suppress our own idiosyncrasy without impoverishing it. But as time goes on perhaps we can train our taste; perhaps we can make it submit to some control. When it has fed greedily and

lavishly upon books of all sorts—poetry, fiction, history, biography—and has stopped reading and looked for long spaces upon the variety, the incongruity of the living world, we shall find that it is changing a little; it is not so greedy, it is more reflective. It will begin to bring us not merely judgments on particular books, but it will tell us that there is a quality common to certain books.

For Woolf, independence is the most important quality a reader can possess. Critics are only able to help us

if we come to them laden with questions and suggestions won honestly in the course of our own reading. They can do nothing for us if we herd ourselves under their authority and lie down like sheep in the shade of a hedge. We can only understand their ruling when it comes in conflict with our own and vanquishes it.

In 1928, Virginia Woolf was invited to lecture on "Women and Fiction" at two women's colleges at Cambridge University. A year later she published the revised and expanded lectures as A Room of One's Own. *In the first chapter she describes a nameless young woman's visit to "Oxbridge," an imaginary university. After lunching richly at Oxbridge with the men and sharing a poor dinner at the women's college, she begins to wonder: Why are women poor? And what effect does poverty—and the resulting "lack of tradition"—have on the mind? In chapter two, our selection, the young woman pursues these questions in the public reading room of the British Museum and develops a theory to explain the inferior position of women in society.*

A Room of One's Own

Virginia Woolf

The scene, if I may ask you to follow me, was now changed. The leaves were still falling, but in London now, not Oxbridge; and I must ask you to imagine a room, like many thousands, with a window looking across people's hats and vans and motor-cars to other windows, and on the table inside the room a blank sheet of paper on which was written in large letters WOMEN AND FICTION, but no more. The inevitable sequel to lunching and dining at Oxbridge seemed, unfortunately, to be a visit to the British Museum. One must strain off what was personal and accidental in all these impressions and so reach the pure fluid, the essential oil of truth. For that visit to Oxbridge and the luncheon and the dinner had started a swarm of questions. Why did men drink wine and women water? Why was one sex so prosperous and the other so poor? What effect has poverty on fiction? What conditions are necessary for the creation of works of art?—a thousand questions at once sug-

---

*A selection from *A Room of One's Own*.

gested themselves. But one needed answers, not questions; and an answer was only to be had by consulting the learned and the unprejudiced, who have removed themselves above the strife of tongue and the confusion of body and issued the result of their reasoning and research in books which are to be found in the British Museum. If truth is not to be found on the shelves of the British Museum, where, I asked myself, picking up a notebook and a pencil, is truth?

Thus provided, thus confident and enquiring, I set out in the pursuit of truth. The day, though not actually wet, was dismal, and the streets in the neighborhood of the Museum were full of open coal-holes, down which sacks were showering; four-wheeled cabs were drawing up and depositing on the pavement corded boxes containing, presumably, the entire wardrobe of some Swiss or Italian family seeking fortune or refuge or some other desirable commodity which is to be found in the boarding-houses of Bloomsbury in the winter. The usual hoarse-voiced men paraded the streets with plants on barrows. Some shouted; others sang. London was like a workshop. London was like a machine. We were all being shot backwards and forwards on this plain foundation to make some pattern. The British Museum was another department of the factory. The swing-doors swung open; and there one stood under the vast dome, as if one were a thought in the huge bald forehead which is so splendidly encircled by a band of famous names. One went to the counter; one took a slip of paper; one opened a volume of the catalogue, and . . . . . the five dots here indicate five separate minutes of stupefaction, wonder and bewilderment. Have you any notion how many books are written about women in the course of one year? Have you any notion how many are written by men? Are you aware that you are, perhaps, the most discussed animal in the universe? Here had I come with a notebook and a pencil proposing to spend a morning reading, supposing that at the end of the morning I should have transferred the truth to my notebook. But I should need to be a herd of elephants, I thought, and a wilderness of spiders, desperately referring to the animals that are reputed longest lived and most multitudinously eyed, to cope with all this. I should need claws of steel and beak of brass even to penetrate the husk. How shall I ever find the grains of truth embedded in all this mass of paper, I asked myself, and in despair began running my eye up and down the long list of titles. Even the names of the books gave me food for thought. Sex and its nature might well attract doctors and biologists; but what was surprising and difficult of explanation was the fact that sex—woman, that is to say—also attracts agreeable essayists, light-fingered novelists, young men who have taken the M.A. degree; men who have taken no degree; men who have no apparent qualification save that they are not women. Some of these books were, on the face of it, frivolous and facetious; but many, on the other hand, were serious and prophetic, moral and hortatory. Merely to read the titles suggested innumerable schoolmasters, innumerable clergymen mounting their platforms and pulpits and holding forth with a loquacity which far exceeded the hour usually allotted to such discourse on this one subject. It was a most strange phenomenon; and apparently—here I consulted the letter M—one confined to male sex. Women do not write books about men—a fact that I could not help welcoming with relief, for if I had first to read all that men have written about women, then all that women have written about men, the aloe that flowers once in a hundred years would flower twice before I could set pen to paper. So, making a perfectly arbitrary choice of a dozen volumes or so, I sent my slips of paper to lie in the wire tray, and waited in my stall, among the other seekers for the essential oil of truth.

What could be the reason, then, of this curious disparity, I wondered, drawing cartwheels on the slips of paper provided by the British taxpayer for other purposes. Why are women, judging from this catalogue, so much more interesting to men than men are to women? A very curious fact it seemed, and my mind wandered to picture the lives of men who spend their time in writing books about women; whether they were old or young, married or unmarried, red-nosed or hump-backed—anyhow, it was flattering, vaguely, to feel oneself the object of such attention, provided that it was not entirely bestowed by the crippled and the infirm—so I pondered until all such frivolous thoughts were ended by an avalanche of books sliding down on to the desk in front of me. Now the trouble began. The student who has been trained in research at Oxbridge has no doubt some method of shepherding his question past all distractions till it runs into its answer as a sheep runs into its pen. The student by my side, for instance, who was copying assiduously from a scientific manual was, I felt sure, extracting pure nuggets of the essential ore every ten minutes or so. His little grunts of satisfaction indicated so much. But if, unfortunately, one has had no training in a university, the question far from being shepherded to its pen flies like a frightened flock hither and thither, helter-skelter, pursued by a whole pack of hounds. Professors, schoolmasters, sociologists, clergymen, novelists, essayists, journalists, men who had no qualification save that they were not women, chased my simple and single question—Why are women poor?—until it became fifty questions; until the fifty questions leapt frantically into mid-stream and were carried away. Every page in my notebook was scribbled over with notes. To show the state of mind I was in, I will read you a few of them, explaining that the page was headed quite simply, WOMEN AND POVERTY, in block letters; but what followed was something like this:

Condition in Middle Ages of,
Habits in the Fiji Islands of,
Worshipped as goddesses by,
Weaker in moral sense than,
Idealism of,
Greater conscientiousness of,
South Sea Islanders, age of puberty among,
Attractiveness of,
Offered as sacrifice to,
Small size of brain of,
Profounder sub-consciousness of,
Less hair on the body of,
Mental, moral and physical inferiority of,
Love of children of,
Greater length of life of,
Weaker muscles of,
Strength of affections of,
Vanity of,
Higher education of,
Shakespeare's opinion of,
Lord Birkenhead's opinion of,
Dean Inge's opinion of,
La Bruyère's opinion of,
Dr. Johnson's opinion of,
Mr. Oscar Browning's opinion of, . . .

Here I drew breath and added, indeed, in the margin, Why does Samuel Butler say, "Wise men never say what they think of women"? Wise men never say anything else apparently. But, I continued, leaning back in my chair and looking at the vast dome in which I was a single but by now somewhat harassed thought, what is so unfortunate is that wise men never think the same thing about women. Here is Pope:

Most women have no character at all.

And here is La Bruyère:

> Les femmes sont extrêmes; elles sont meilleures ou pires que les
> hommes [women are the extremes; they are better or worse than
> men]—

a direct contradiction by keen observers who were contemporary. Are they capable of education or incapable? Napoleon
thought them incapable. Dr. Johnson thought the opposite.*
Have they souls or have they not souls? Some savages say they
have none. Others, on the contrary, maintain that women are
half divine and worship them on that account.† Some sages
hold that they are shallower in the brain; others that they are
deeper in the consciousness. Goethe honoured them; Mussolini despises them. Wherever one looked men thought about
women and thought differently. It was impossible to make
head or tail of it all, I decided, glancing with envy at the reader
next door who was making the neatest abstracts, headed often
with an A or a B or a C, while my own notebook rioted with
the wildest scribble of contradictory jottings. It was distressing,
it was bewildering, it was humiliating. Truth had run through
my fingers. Every drop had escaped.

I could not possibly go home, I reflected, and add as a
serious contribution to the study of women and fiction that
women have less hair on their bodies than men, or that the age
of puberty among the South Sea Islanders is nine—or is it
ninety?—even the handwriting had become in its distraction
indecipherable. It was disgraceful to have nothing more weighty

---

* " 'Men know that women are an overmatch for them, and therefore
they choose the weakest or the most ignorant. If they did not think so, they
never could be afraid of women knowing as much as themselves.' . . . In
justice to the sex, I think it but candid to acknowledge that, in a subsequent
conversation, he told me that he was serious in what he said."—BOSWELL,
The Journal of a Tour to the Hebrides.

† "The ancient Germans believed that there was something holy in
women, and accordingly consulted them as oracles."—FRAZER, *Golden
Bough.*

or respectable to show after a whole morning's work. And if I could not grasp the truth about W. (as for brevity's sake I had come to call her) in the past, why bother about W. in the future? It seemed pure waste of time to consult all those gentlemen who specialise in woman and her effect on whatever it may be—politics, children, wages, morality—numerous and learned as they are. One might as well leave their books unopened.

But while I pondered I had unconsciously, in my listlessness, in my desperation, been drawing a picture where I should, like my neighbour, have been writing a conclusion. I had been drawing a face, a figure. It was the face and the figure of Professor von X. engaged in writing his monumental work entitled *The Mental, Moral, and Physical Inferiority of the Female Sex*. He was not in my picture a man attractive to women. He was heavily built; he had a great jowl; to balance that he had very small eyes; he was very red in the face. His expression suggested that he was labouring under some emotion that made him jab his pen on the paper as if he were killing some noxious insect as he wrote, but even when he had killed it that did not satisfy him; he must go on killing it; and even so, some cause for anger and irritation remained. Could it be his wife, I asked, looking at my picture. Was she in love with a cavalry officer? Was the cavalry officer slim and elegant and dressed in astrachan? Had he been laughed at, to adopt the Freudian theory, in his cradle by a pretty girl? For even in his cradle the professor, I thought, could not have been an attractive child. Whatever the reason, the professor was made to look very angry and very ugly in my sketch, as he wrote his great book upon the mental, moral and physical inferiority of women. Drawing pictures was an idle way of finishing an unprofitable morning's work. Yet it is in our idleness, in our dreams, that the submerged truth sometimes comes to the top. A very elementary exercise in psychology, not to be dignified by the name of psycho-analysis, showed me, on looking at my note-book, that the sketch of the angry professor had been made in anger. Anger had snatched my pencil while I dreamt. But what was anger doing there? Interest, confusion, amusement, bore-dom—all these emotions I could trace and name as they suc-ceeded each other throughout the morning. Had anger, the black snake, been lurking among them? Yes, said the sketch, anger had. It referred me unmistakably to the one book, to the one phrase, which had roused the demon; it was the professor's statement about the mental, moral and physical inferiority of women. My heart had leapt. My cheeks had burnt. I had flushed with anger. There was nothing specially remarkable, however foolish, in that. One does not like to be told that one is naturally the inferior of a little man—I looked at the student next me—who breathes hard, wears a ready-made tie, and has not shaved this fortnight. One has certain foolish vanities. It is only human nature, I reflected, and began drawing cart-wheels and circles over the angry professor's face till he looked like a burning bush or a flaming comet—anyhow, an appari-tion without human semblance or significance. The professor was nothing now but a faggot burning on the top of Hampstead Heath. Soon my own anger was explained and done with; but curiosity remained. How explain the anger of the professors? Why were they angry? For when it came to analysing the impression left by these books there was always an element of heat. This heat took many forms; it showed itself in satire, in sentiment, in curiosity, in reprobation. But there was another element which was often present and could not immediately be identified. Anger, I called it. But it was anger that had gone underground and mixed itself with all kinds of other emotions. To judge from its odd effects, it was anger disguised and com-plex, not anger simple and open.

Whatever the reason, all these books, I thought, surveying the pile on the desk, are worthless for my purposes. They were worthless scientifically, that is to say, though humanly they were full of instruction, interest, boredom, and very queer facts about the habits of the Fiji Islanders. They had been written in the red light of emotion and not in the white light of truth. Therefore they must be returned to the central desk and restored each to his own cell in the enormous honeycomb. All that I had retrieved from that morning's work had been the one fact of anger. The professors—I lumped them together thus—were angry. But why, I asked myself, having returned the books, why, I repeated, standing under the colonnade among the pigeons and the prehistoric canoes, why are they angry? And, asking myself this question, I strolled off to find a place for luncheon. What is the real nature of what I call for the moment their anger? I asked. Here was a puzzle that would last all the time that it takes to be served with food in a small restaurant somewhere near the British Museum. Some previous luncher had left the lunch edition of the evening paper on a chair, and, waiting to be served, I began idly reading the headlines. A ribbon of very large letters ran across the page. Somebody had made a big score in South Africa. Lesser ribbons announced that Sir Austen Chamberlain was at Geneva. A meat axe with human hair on it had been found in a cellar. Mr. Justice———— commented in the Divorce Courts upon the Shamelessness of Women. Sprinkled about the paper were other pieces of news. A film actress had been lowered from a peak in California and hung suspended in mid-air. The weather was going to be foggy. The most transient visitor to this planet, I thought, who picked up this paper could not fail to be aware, even from this scattered testimony, that England is under the rule of a patriarchy. Nobody in their senses could fail to detect the dominance of the professor. His was the power and the money and the influence. He was the proprietor of the paper and its editor and sub-editor. He was the Foreign Secretary and the Judge. He was the cricketer; he owned the racehorses and the yachts. He was the director of the company that pays two hundred per cent to its shareholders. He left millions to charities and colleges that were ruled by himself. He suspended the film actress in mid-air. He will decide if the hair on the meat axe is human; he it is who will acquit or convict the murderer, and hang him, or let him go free. With the exception of the fog he seemed to control everything. Yet he was angry. I knew that he was angry by this token. When I read what he wrote about women I thought, not of what he was saying, but of himself. When an arguer argues dispassionately he thinks only of the argument; and the reader cannot help thinking of the argument too. If he had written dispassionately about women, had used indisputable proofs to establish his argument and had shown no trace of wishing that the result should be one thing rather than another, one would not have been angry either. One would have accepted the fact, as one accepts the fact that a pea is green or a canary yellow. So be it, I should have said. But I had been angry because he was angry. Yet it seemed absurd, I thought, turning over the evening paper, that a man with all this power should be angry. Or is anger, I wondered, somehow, the familiar, the attendant sprite on power? Rich people, for example, are often angry because they suspect that the poor want to seize their wealth. The professors, or patriarchs, as it might be more accurate to call them, might be angry for that reason partly, but partly for one that lies a little less obviously on the surface. Possibly they were not "angry" at all; often, indeed, they were admiring, devoted, exemplary in the relations of private life. Possibly when the professor insisted a little too emphatically upon the inferiority of women, he was concerned not with their inferiority, but with his own superiority. That was what he was protecting rather hot-headedly and with too much emphasis, because it was a jewel to him of the rarest price. Life for both sexes—and I looked at them, shouldering their way along the pavement—is arduous, difficult, a perpetual struggle. It calls for gigantic courage and strength. More than anything, perhaps, creatures of illusion as we are, it calls for confidence in oneself. Without self-confidence we are as babes in the cradle. And how can we generate this imponderable quality, which is yet so invaluable, most quickly? By thinking that other people are inferior to oneself. By feeling that one has some innate superiority—it may be wealth, or rank, a straight nose, or the portrait of a grandfather by Romney—for there is no end to the pathetic devices of the human imagination—over other people. Hence the enormous importance to a patriarch who has to conquer, who has to rule, of feeling that great numbers of people, half the human race indeed, are by nature inferior to himself. It must indeed be one of the chief sources of his power. But let me turn the light of this observation on to real life, I thought. Does it help to explain some of those psychological puzzles that one notes in the margin of daily life? Does it explain my astonishment the other day when Z, most humane, most modest of men, taking up some book by Rebecca West and reading a passage in it, exclaimed, "The arrant feminist! She says that men are snobs!" The exclamation, to me so surprising—for why was Miss West an arrant feminist for making a possibly true if uncomplimentary statement about the other sex?—was not merely the cry of wounded vanity; it was a protest against some infringement of his power to believe in himself. Women have served all these centuries as looking-glasses possessing the magic and delicious power of reflecting the figure of man at twice its natural size. Without that power probably the earth would still be swamp and jungle. The glories of all our wars would be unknown. We should still be scratching the outlines of deer on the remains of mutton bones and bartering flints for sheepskins or whatever simple ornament took our unsophisticated taste. Supermen and Fingers of Destiny would never have existed. The Czar and the Kaiser would never have worn their crowns or lost them. Whatever may be their use in civilised societies, mirrors are essential to all violent and heroic action. That is why Napoleon and Mussolini both insist so emphatically upon the inferiority of women, for if they were not inferior, they would cease to enlarge. That serves to explain in part the necessity that women so often are to men. And it serves to explain how restless they are under her criticism; how impossible it is for her to say to them this book is bad, this picture is feeble, or whatever it may be, without giving far more pain and rousing far more anger than a man would do who gave the same criticism. For if she begins to tell the truth, the figure in the looking-glass shrinks; his fitness for life is diminished. How is he to go on giving judgement, civilising natives, making laws, writing books, dressing up and speechifying at banquets, unless he can see himself at breakfast and at dinner at least twice the size he really is? So I reflected, crumbling my bread and stirring my coffee and now and again looking at the people in the street. The looking-glass vision is of supreme importance because it charges the vitality; it stimulates the nervous system. Take it away and man may die, like the drug fiend deprived of his cocaine. Under the spell of that illusion, I thought, looking out of the window, half the people on the pavement are striding to work. They put on their hats and coats in the morning under its agreeable rays. They start the day confident, braced, believing themselves desired at Miss Smith's tea party; they say to themselves as they go into the room, I am the superior of half the people here, and it is thus that they speak with that self-confidence, that self-assurance, which have had such profound consequences in public life and lead to such curious notes in the margin of the private mind.

But these contributions to the dangerous and fascinating subject of the psychology of the other sex—it is one, I hope, that you will investigate when you have five hundred a year of your own—were interrupted by the necessity of paying the bill. It came to five shillings and ninepence. I gave the waiter a ten-shilling note and he went to bring me change. There was another ten-shilling note in my purse; I noticed it, because it is a fact that still takes my breath away—the power of my purse to breed ten-shilling notes automatically. I open it and there they are. Society gives me chicken and coffee, bed and lodging, in return for a certain number of pieces of paper which were left me by an aunt, for no other reason than that I share her name.

My aunt, Mary Beton, I must tell you, died by a fall from her horse when she was riding out to take the air in Bombay. The news of my legacy reached me one night about the same time that the act was passed that gave votes to women. A solicitor's letter fell into the post-box and when I opened it I found that she had left me five hundred pounds a year for ever. Of the two—the vote and the money—the money, I own, seemed infinitely the more important. Before that I had made my living by cadging odd jobs from newspapers, by reporting a donkey show here or a wedding there; I had earned a few pounds by addressing envelopes, reading to old ladies, making artifical flowers, teaching the alphabet to small children in a kindergarten. Such were the chief occupations that were open to women before 1918. I need not, I am afraid, describe in any detail the hardness of the work, for you know perhaps women who have done it; nor the difficulty of living on the money when it was earned, for you may have tried. But what still remains with me as a worse infliction than either was the poison of fear and bitterness which those days bred in me. To begin with, always to be doing work that one did not wish to do, and to do it like a slave, flattering and fawning, not always necessarily perhaps, but it seemed necessary and the stakes were too great to run risks; and then the thought of that one gift which it was death to hide—a small one but dear to the possessor—perishing and with it myself, my soul—all this became like a rust eating away the bloom of the spring, destroying the tree at its heart. However, as I say, my aunt died; and whenever I change a ten-shilling note a little of that rust and corrosion is rubbed off; fear and bitterness go. Indeed, I thought, slipping the silver into my purse, it is remarkable, remembering the bitterness of those days, what a change of temper a fixed income will bring about. No force in the world can take from me my five hundred pounds. Food, house and clothing are mine for ever. Therefore not merely do effort and labour cease, but also hatred and bitterness. I need not hate any man; he cannot hurt me. I need not flatter any man; he has nothing to give me. So imperceptibly I found myself adopting a new attitude towards the other half of the human race. It was absurd to blame any class or any sex, as a whole. Great bodies of people are never responsible for what they do. They are driven by instincts which are not within their control. They too, the patriarchs, the professors, had endless difficulties, terrible drawbacks to contend with. Their education had been in some ways as faulty as my own. It had bred in them defects as great. True, they had money and power, but only at the cost of harboring in their breasts an eagle, a vulture, for ever tearing the liver out and plucking at the lungs—the instinct for possession, the rage for acquisition which drives them to desire other people's fields and goods perpetually; to make frontiers and flags; battleships and poison gas; to offer up their own lives and their children's lives. Walk through the Admiralty Arch

(I had reached that monument), or any other avenue given up to trophies and cannon, and reflect upon the kind of glory celebrated there. Or watch in the spring sunshine the stockbroker and the great barrister going indoors to make money and more money and more money when it is a fact that five hundred pounds a year will keep one alive in the sunshine. These are unpleasant instincts to harbour, I reflected. They are bred of the conditions of life; of the lack of civilisation, I thought, looking at the statue of the Duke of Cambridge, and in particular at the feathers in his cocked hat, with a fixity that they have scarcely ever received before. And, as I realised these drawbacks, by degrees fear and bitterness modified themselves into pity and toleration; and then in a year or two, pity and toleration went, and the greatest release of all came, which is freedom to think of things in themselves. That building, for example, do I like it or not? Is that picture beautiful or not? Is that in my opinion a good book or a bad? Indeed my aunt's legacy unveiled the sky to me, and substituted for the large and imposing figure of a gentleman, which Milton recommended for my perpetual adoration, a view of the open sky.

So thinking, so speculating, I found my way back to my house by the river. Lamps were being lit and an indescribable change had come over London since the morning hour. It was as if the great machine after labouring all day had made with our help a few yards of something very exciting and beautiful—a fiery fabric flashing with red eyes, a tawny monster roaring with hot breath. Even the wind seemed flung like a flag as it lashed the houses and rattled the hoardings.

In my little street, however, domesticity prevailed. The house painter was descending his ladder; the nursemaid was wheeling the perambulator carefully in and out back to nursery tea; the coal-heaver was folding his empty sacks on top of each other; the woman who keeps the green-grocer's shop was adding up the day's takings with her hands in red mittens. But so engrossed was I with the problem you have laid upon my shoulders that I could not see even these usual sights without referring them to one centre. I thought how much harder it is now than it must have been even a century ago to say which of these employments is the higher, the more necessary. Is it better to be a coal-heaver or a nursemaid; is the charwoman who has brought up eight children of less value to the world than the barrister who has made a hundred thousand pounds? It is useless to ask such questions; for nobody can answer them. Not only do the comparative values of charwomen and lawyers rise and fall from decade to decade, but we have no rods with which to measure them even as they are at the moment. I had been foolish to ask my professor to furnish me with "indisputable proofs" of this or that in his argument about women. Even if one could state the value of any one gift at the moment, those values will change; in a century's time very possibly they will have changed completely. Moreover, in a hundred years, I thought, reaching my own doorstep, women will have ceased to be the protected sex. Logically they will take part in all the activities and exertions that were once denied them. The nursemaid will heave coal. The shop-woman will drive an engine. All assumptions founded on the facts observed when women were the protected sex will have disappeared—as, for example (here a squad of soldiers marched down the street), that women and clergymen and gardeners live longer than other people. Remove that protection, expose them to the same exertions and activities, make them soldiers and sailors and engine-drivers and dock labourers, and will not women die off so much younger, so much quicker, than men that one will say, "I saw a woman today," as one used to say, "I saw an aeroplane." Anything may happen when womanhood has ceased to be a protected occupation, I thought, opening the door. But what bearing has all this upon the subject of my paper, Women and Fiction? I asked, going indoors.

Interpretive Questions

1. According to Woolf, why are opinions about women so contradictory?

2. Why does Woolf go to the British Museum when she doesn't expect to find what she's looking for there?

3. Does Woolf think women should not have served as magnifying mirrors for men?

4. Why doesn't Woolf blame men for the condition of women?

5. Does Woolf think the self-confidence necessary for success must be based on an illusion? p. 130

XII

By and About Delmore Schwartz

(1913–1966)

Delmore Schwartz was deeply concerned about the poet's position in contemporary American society. A poet himself, he wrote about his vocation:

> The distinguishing mark of the poet, that aptitude which more than any other skill of the mind makes him a poet, is metaphor. . . . Now metaphor is literally a bearing-across, or a bringing-together of things by means of words. And composition, which is what the poet accomplishes by all the elements of his poem when they are brought together in a unity, structural, formal, intuitive, and musical—composition means putting things together, bringing them together into a unity which is original, interesting, and fruitful. Thus the poet at any time may be said to be engaged in bringing things together, in making new things, in uniting the old and the new, all by the inexhaustible means which words provide for him.

According to Schwartz, one must have a sense of the past in order to understand the present:

> And one must have a strong sense of actuality in order to know just what of the past is alive in the present and what is merely a monument or a souvenir. Without a sense of the past, one's sense of the actual is likely to be confused with an obsessive pursuit of what is degraded, or idiosyncratic, or transitory, or brand-new. . . . Conversely, a sense of the actual enables one to understand the past itself as something which was not by any means Arcadian. Perhaps one can go so far as to say that one cannot have much of a sense of the past without a sense of the actual or much of a sense of the actual without a sense of the past.

In Dreams Begin Responsibilities

Delmore Schwartz

I

I think it is the year 1909. I feel as if I were in a motion picture theatre, the long arm of light crossing the darkness and spinning, my eyes fixed on the screen. This is a silent picture as if an old Biograph one, in which the actors are dressed in ridiculously old-fashioned clothes, and one flash succeeds another with sudden jumps. The actors too seem to jump about and walk too fast. The shots themselves are full of dots and rays, as if it were raining when the picture was photographed. The light is bad.

It is Sunday afternoon, June 12th, 1909, and my father is walking down the quiet streets of Brooklyn on his way to visit my mother. His clothes are newly pressed and his tie is too tight in his collar. He jingles the coins in his pockets, thinking of the witty things he will say. I feel as if I had by now relaxed entirely in the soft darkness of the theatre; the organist peals out the obvious and approximate emotions on which the audience rocks unknowingly. I am anonymous, and I have forgotten myself. It is always so when one goes to the movies, it is, as they say, a drug.

My father walks from street to street of trees, lawns and houses, once in a while coming to an avenue on which a streetcar skates and gnaws, slowly progressing. The conductor, who has a handle-bar mustache, helps a young lady wearing a hat like a bowl with feathers on to the car. She lifts her long skirts slightly as she mounts the steps. He leisurely makes change and rings his bell. It is obviously Sunday, for everyone is wearing Sunday clothes, and the streetcar's noises emphasize the quiet of the holiday. Is not Brooklyn the City of Churches? The shops are closed and their shades drawn, but for an occasional stationery store or drugstore with great green balls in the window.

My father has chosen to take this long walk because he likes to walk and think. He thinks about himself in the future and so arrives at the place he is to visit in a state of mild exaltation. He pays no attention to the houses he is passing, in which the Sunday dinner is being eaten, nor to the many trees which patrol each street, now coming to their full leafage and the time when they will room the whole street in cool shadow. An occasional carriage passes, the horse's hooves falling like stones in the quiet afternoon, and once in a while an automobile, looking like an enormous upholstered sofa, puffs and passes.

My father thinks of my mother, of how nice it will be to introduce her to his family. But he is not yet sure that he wants to marry her, and once in a while he becomes panicky about the bond already established. He reassures himself by thinking of the big men he admires who are married: William Randolph Hearst, and William Howard Taft, who had just become President of the United States.

My father arrives at my mother's house. He has come too

early and so is suddenly embarrassed. My aunt, my mother's sister, answers the loud bell with her napkin in her hand, for the family is still at dinner. As my father enters, my grandfather rises from the table and shakes hands with him. My mother has run upstairs to tidy herself. My grandmother asks my father if he has had dinner, and tells him that Rose will be downstairs soon. My grandfather opens the conversation by remarking on the mild June weather. My father sits uncomfortably near the table, holding his hat in his hand. My grandmother tells my aunt to take my father's hat. My uncle, twelve years old, runs into the house, his hair tousled. He shouts a greeting to my father, who has often given him a nickel, and then runs upstairs. It is evident that the respect in which my father is held in this household is tempered by a good deal of mirth. He is impressive, yet he is very awkward.

II

Finally my mother comes downstairs, all dressed up, and my father being engaged in conversation with my grandfather becomes uneasy, not knowing whether to greet my mother or continue the conversation. He gets up from the chair clumsily and says "hello" gruffly. My grandfather watches, examining their congruence, such as it is, with a critical eye, and meanwhile rubbing his bearded cheek roughly, as he always does when he reflects. He is worried; he is afraid that my father will not make a good husband for his oldest daughter. At this point something happens to the film, just as my father is saying something funny to my mother; I am awakened to myself and my unhappiness just as my interest was rising. The audience begins to clap impatiently. Then the trouble is cared for but the film has been returned to a portion just shown, and once more I see my grandfather rubbing his bearded cheek and pondering my father's character. It is difficult to get back into the picture once more and forget myself, but as my mother giggles at my father's words, the darkness drowns me.

My father and mother depart from the house, my father shaking hands with my mother once more, out of some un-known uneasiness. I stir uneasily also, slouched in the hard chair of the theatre. Where is the older uncle, my mother's older brother? He is studying in his bedroom upstairs, studying for his final examination at the College of the City of New York, having been dead of rapid pneumonia for the last twenty-one years. My mother and father walk down the same quiet streets once more. My mother is holding my father's arm and telling him of the novel which she has been reading; and my father utters judgments of the characters as the plot is made clear to him. This is a habit which he very much enjoys, for he feels the utmost superiority and confidence when he ap-proves and condemns the behavior of other people. At times he feels moved to utter a brief "Ugh"—whenever the story becomes what he would call sugary. This tribute is paid to his manliness. My mother feels satisfied by the interest which she has awakened; she is showing my father how intelligent she is, and how interesting.

They reach the avenue, and the streetcar leisurely arrives. They are going to Coney Island this afternoon, although my mother considers that such pleasures are inferior. She has made up her mind to indulge only in a walk on the boardwalk and a pleasant dinner, avoiding the riotous amusements as being beneath the dignity of so dignified a couple.

My father tells my mother how much money he has made in the past week, exaggerating an amount which need not have been exaggerated. But my father has always felt that actualities somehow fall short. Suddenly I begin to weep. The deter-mined old lady who sits next to me in the theatre is annoyed and looks at me with an angry face, and being intimidated, I stop. I drag out my handkerchief and dry my face, licking the drop which has fallen near my lips. Meanwhile I have missed something, for here are my mother and father alighting at the last stop, Coney Island.

III

They walk toward the boardwalk, and my father commands my mother to inhale the pungent air from the sea. They both breathe in deeply, both of them laughing as they do so. They have in common a great interest in health, although my father is strong and husky, my mother frail. Their minds are full of theories of what is good to eat and not good to eat, and sometimes they engage in heated discussions of the subject, the whole matter ending in my father's announcement, made with a scornful bluster, that you have to die sooner or later anyway. On the boardwalk's flagpole, the American flag is pulsing in an intermittent wind from the sea.

My father and mother go to the rail of the boardwalk and look down on the beach where a good many bathers are casually walking about. A few are in the surf. A peanut whistle pierces the air with its pleasant and active whine, and my father goes to buy peanuts. My mother remains at the rail and stares at the ocean. The ocean seems merry to her; it pointedly sparkles and again and again the pony waves are released. She notices the children digging in the wet sand, and the bathing costumes of the girls who are her own age. My father returns with the peanuts. Overhead the sun's lightning strikes and strikes, but neither of them are at all aware of it. The boardwalk is full of people dressed in their Sunday clothes and idly strolling. The tide does not reach as far as the boardwalk, and the strollers would feel no danger if it did. My mother and father lean on the rail of the boardwalk and absently stare at the ocean. The ocean is becoming rough; the waves come in slowly, tugging strength from far back. The moment before they somersault, the moment when they arch their backs so beautifully, showing green and white veins amid the black, that moment is intolerable. They finally crack, dashing fiercely upon the sand, actually driving, full force downward, against the sand, bouncing upward and forward, and at last petering out into a small stream which races up the beach and then is recalled. My parents gaze absentmindedly at the ocean, scarcely interested in its harshness. The sun overhead does not disturb them. But I stare at the terrible sun which breaks up sight, and the fatal, merciless, passionate ocean, I forget my parents. I stare fascinated and finally, shocked by the indifference of my father and mother, I burst out weeping once more. The old lady next to me pats me on the shoulder and says "There, there, all of this is only a movie, young man, only a movie," but I look up once more at the terrifying sun and the terrifying ocean, and being unable to control my tears, I get up and go to the men's room, stumbling over the feet of the other people seated in my row.

IV

When I return, feeling as if I had awakened in the morning sick for lack of sleep, several hours have apparently passed and my parents are riding on the merry-go-round. My father is on a black horse, my mother on a white one, and they seem to be making an eternal circuit for the single purpose of snatching the nickel rings which are attached to the arm of one of the posts. A hand organ is playing; it is one with the ceaseless circling of the merry-go-round.

For a moment it seems that they will never get off the merry-go-round because it will never stop. I feel like one who looks down on the avenue from the 50th story of a building. But at length they do get off; even the music of the hand organ has ceased for a moment. My father has acquired ten rings, my mother only two, although it was my mother who really wanted them.

They walk on along the boardwalk as the afternoon descends by imperceptible degrees into the incredible violet of dusk. Everything fades into a relaxed glow, even the ceaseless murmuring from the beach, and the revolutions of the merry-go-round. They look for a place to have dinner. My father suggests the best one on the boardwalk and my mother demurs, in accordance with her principles.

However they do go to the best place, asking for a table near the window, so that they can look out on the boardwalk and the mobile ocean. My father feels omnipotent as he places a quarter in the waiter's hand as he asks for a table. The place is crowded and here too there is music, this time from a kind of string trio. My father orders dinner with a fine confidence.

As the dinner is eaten, my father tells of his plans for the future, and my mother shows with expressive face how interested she is, and how impressed. My father becomes exultant. He is lifted up by the waltz that is being played, and his own future begins to intoxicate him. My father tells my mother that he is going to expand his business, for there is a great deal of money to be made. He wants to settle down. After all, he is twenty-nine, he has lived by himself since he was thirteen, he is making more and more money, and he is envious of his married friends when he visits them in the cozy security of their homes, surrounded, it seems, by the calm domestic pleasures, and by delightful children, and then, as the waltz reaches the moment when all the dancers swing madly, then, then with awful daring, then he asks my mother to marry him, although awkwardly enough and puzzled, even in his excitement, at how he had arrived at the proposal, and she, to make the whole business worse, begins to cry, and my father looks nervously about, not knowing at all what to do now, and my mother says: "It's all I've wanted from the moment I saw you," sobbing, and he finds all of this very difficult, scarcely to his taste, scarcely as he had thought it would be, on his long walks over Brooklyn Bridge in the revery of a fine cigar, and it was then that I stood up in the theatre and shouted: "Don't do it. It's not too late to change your minds, both of you. Nothing good will come of it, only remorse, hatred, scandal, and two children whose characters are monstrous." The whole audience turned to look at me, annoyed, the usher came hurrying down the aisle flashing his searchlight, and the old lady next to me tugged me down into my seat, saying: "Be quiet. You'll be put out, and you paid thirty-five cents to come in." And so I shut my eyes because I could not bear to see what was happening. I sat there quietly.

V

But after a while I begin to take brief glimpses, and at length I watch again with thirsty interest, like a child who wants to maintain his sulk although offered the bribe of candy. My parents are now having their picture taken in a photographer's booth along the boardwalk. The place is shadowed in the mauve light which is apparently necessary. The camera is set to the side on its tripod and looks like a Martian man. The photographer is instructing my parents in how to pose. My father has his arm over my mother's shoulder, and both of them smile emphatically. The photographer brings my mother a bouquet of flowers to hold in her hand but she holds it at the wrong angle. Then the photographer covers himself with the black cloth which drapes the camera and all that one sees of him is one protruding arm and his hand which clutches the rubber ball which he will squeeze when the picture is finally taken. But he is not satisfied with their appearance. He feels with certainty that somehow there is something wrong in their pose. Again and again he issues from his hidden place with new directions. Each suggestion merely makes matters worse. My father is becoming impatient. They try a seated pose. The photographer explains that he has pride, he is not interested in all of this for the money, he wants to make beautiful pictures. My father says: "Hurry up, will you? We haven't got all night." But the photographer only scurries about apologetically, and issues new directions. The photographer charms me. I approve of him with all my heart, for I know just how he feels, and as he criticizes each revised pose according to some unknown idea of rightness, I become quite hopeful. But then my father says angrily: "Come on, you've had enough time, we're not going to wait any longer." And the photographer, sighing unhappily, goes back under his black covering, holds out his hand, says: "One, two, three, Now!", and the picture is taken, with my father's smile turned to a grimace and my mother's bright and false. It takes a few minutes for the picture to be developed and as my parents sit in the curious light they become quite depressed.

VI

They have passed a fortune-teller's booth, and my mother wishes to go in, but my father does not. They begin to argue about it. My mother becomes stubborn, my father once more impatient, and then they begin to quarrel, and what my father would like to do is walk off and leave my mother there, but he knows that that would never do. My mother refuses to budge. She is near to tears, but she feels an uncontrollable desire to hear what the palm-reader will say. My father consents angrily, and they both go into a booth which is in a way like the photographer's, since it is draped in black cloth and its light is shadowed. The place is too warm, and my father keeps saying this is all nonsense, pointing to the crystal ball on the table. The fortune-teller, a fat, short woman, garbed in what is supposed to be Oriental robes, comes into the room from the back and greets them, speaking with an accent. But suddenly my father feels that the whole thing is intolerable; he tugs at my mother's arm, but my mother refuses to budge. And then, in terrible anger, my father lets go of my mother's arm and strides out, leaving my mother stunned. She moves to go after my father, but the fortune-teller holds her arm tightly and begs her not to do so, and I in my seat am shocked more than can ever be said, for I feel as if I were walking a tightrope a hundred feet over a circus-audience and suddenly the rope is showing signs of breaking, and I get up from my seat and begin to shout once more the first words I can think of to communicate my terrible fear and once more the usher comes hurrying down the aisle flashing his searchlight and the old lady pleads with me, and the shocked audience has turned to stare at me, and I keep shouting: "What are they doing? Don't they know what they are doing? Why doesn't my mother go after my father? If she does not do that, what will she do? Doesn't my father know what he is doing?"—But the usher has seized my arm and is dragging me away, and as he does so, he says: "What are *you* doing? Don't you know you can't do whatever you want to do? Why should a young man like you, with your whole life before you, get hysterical like this? Why don't you *think* of what you're doing? You can't act like this even if other people aren't around! You will be sorry if you do not do what you should do, you can't carry on like this, it is not right, you will find that out soon enough, everything you do matters too much," and he said that dragging me through the lobby of the theatre into the cold light, and I woke up into the bleak winter morning of my 21st birthday, the windowsill shining with its lip of snow, and the morning already begun.

Interpretive Questions

1. Why does the narrator dream about watching a film? Why is the film about his parents' courtship?

2. Why does the narrator become hysterical and unruly by the end of the film?

3. Why does the narrator feel responsible for the outcome of his parents' dreams?

4. Why is the narrator upset not only when his mother agrees to marry his father, but also when she doesn't follow his father out of the fortune-teller's booth?

5. Why does the film break as it shows the grandfather worrying about the father's suitability as a husband? Why is the scene repeated?